THE 3000-MILE GARDEN

THE
3000-MILE
GARDEN

ROGER PHILLIPS AND LESLIE LAND

an exchange of letters between two eccentric gourmet gardeners; one in London, England, one in Cushing, Maine, U.S.A.

PAN BOOKS

LONDON, SYDNEY AND AUCKLAND

First published 1992 by Pan Books Ltd

a division of Pan Macmillan Publishers Limited
Cavaye Place London SW10 9PG
and Basingstoke

Associated companies throughout the world

ISBN 0 330 32017 3

1 3 5 7 9 8 6 4 2

A CIP catalogue record for this book is available from
the British Library

Photoset by Parker Typesetting Service, Leicester
Printed and bound in Great Britain
by Mackays of Chatham PLC, Chatham, Kent

THE 3000-MILE GARDEN

TOUCH-ME-NOT

MY
BEST
WEEDS

PICK-A-BACK-
PLANT

6 September 1989

Dear Leslie,

I loved your articles in the *New York Times*. You aren't a
garden writer, you're a poet! I have been thinking about you
and your garden and then my mind jumps to what must be
done in my own garden: planting, pruning, trimming,
manuring or just the plain digging up and chucking out.

It was terrific chatting to you up in New Hampshire at the
mushroom bash. Our conversation just got started and then
suddenly it was so late at night that it just got ended, there are
lots of other things I wanted to say but never got round to. I
would like to hear what you are up to and thought you might
like to hear what I am doing in the Eccleston Square garden.
So here are a few more things I wanted to say to you but now
I am going to have to paper speak.

This year the weather in England has been like Egypt: dry,
dry, dry and hot, hot, hot. Watering has been the top
priority. I got back from New England to find that the very
day I had left for a month in the States, 31 July, the water
authority had imposed a hose-pipe ban which has now lasted
over a month and, as we have had no rain at all for the last
three weeks, it looks as if it will be November before we get
the hoses out again.

Let me give you some idea of our garden. It is about three
acres, a typical London square, fenced and locked with what
Thomas Cubitt, the architect, referred to as 'Good iron rail-
ings' in a letter to the then landowner, the Duke of West-
minster, when asking to take a lease on the land to build the
square 'as from Lady Day 1828'.

We have no records of the date the first trees were planted

but I have always supposed that the laying out of the garden would have been concurrent with building the first houses which means 1832 or so. In those days there was only one tree that would grow in the thick, polluted London air: the trees that we call London plane and you call sycamore – *Platanus* × *hispanicus*. (Now the Latin name has changed to *Platanus acerifolia* – these things are sent to try us.) The first plan I can find of the square shows thirty-six trees and the beds, lawns and paths laid out just as they are now. Being an historic area the basic layout of the garden is protected by statute and cannot be interfered with. I don't find this a limitation but an inspiration: it concentrates my mind on the plants and the structures, and forces me to find cunning ways to enhance what is already there. To me a garden should be full of surprises and secrets, areas where you can wander, wonder and generally lose yourself; there should be scents and colours to excite, shapes and textures to stimulate you.

The garden is run by the residents of the square and we each pay a garden rate. At the moment it is £65 per year. The residents elect a committee of twelve to do all the work. I was elected to the committee eight years ago and at the first meeting I attended someone mentioned that I had written books on plants, so they immediately asked me to take over the planting and care of the garden. What they didn't realize was that all my books were on wild flowers and wild plants. I loved the thought of doing it and so did not enlighten them. The garden at that time had just staggered on for years not totally neglected but lacking any loving care. The soil on examination turned out to be dry dust that could not even be watered; water ran off in globules as it does from a duck's back. We were living in a London desert. Large areas had been used for dumping – old leaves, bricks, rubble, cans, bottles, wood, glass, wire – in fact the detritus of the whole period since the beginning of the Second World War. Two gigantic problems needed to be dealt with before planting could be considered: clearing up the rubbish and improving the soil.

I have a theory that bankers, insurance men, stockbrokers and the like are underneath it all frustrated athletes or weight-lifters. I put this to the test by planning a series of Sunday digs. What was really needed was a bulldozer and earth-moving equipment but what I had to hand was city gents. I was right. They all wanted to sweat and ruin their clothes and get generally filthy, moving the fifty or so tons of accumulated rubbish. Under one heap we found all the Tarmac that had been lifted from an ancient tennis court!

In the first area cleared with their sweat I planted a fern garden with a tiny path through the middle. The main ferns are *Matteuccia struthiopteris*, the Shuttlecock Fern, which spreads like mad and *Osmundia regalis*, the Royal Fern. I found a clump of Royal Fern in the New Forest in southern England that was about thirty feet across and seven feet high. My clump is only about six feet across and no more than three feet high at present, despite the fact that we dug out a pit and lined it with plastic to hold the water around it – it thrives in bogs. The ferns do not come into their own until about June so I lined the path with snowdrops and all the surrounds with *Dicentra eximia* supported by a few specimens of *Dicentra spectabilis*, the real Bleeding Heart, to arch over them. On another corner of this bed I have planted a massive clump of blue comfrey, *Symphytum caucasicum*, over-shadowed by an ivy-covered holly. It flowers very early in March when it is only about ten inches high and keeps on flowering until it is about three feet high two months later.

On my travels looking for mushrooms in Washington State, two of the wild plants I saw there stuck in my mind. One was the little Pick-a-Back plant *Tolmiea menziesii*, that grows its new plants from the middle of its leaves – hence its name; and the other was *Aralia spinosa*, the Devil's Walking Stick. The first was easy to get: it is commonly grown as a house plant in England. Anyway I got one and in a few weeks I had propagated about fifty more by just putting mature leaves in pots with a tiny pinch of soil to hold them down. As far as the *Aralia* went, I decided in the end to go for *Aralia elata* 'Variegata', a lovely form of the Japanese angelica tree. Now its gigantic leaves with their multiple leaflets arch gently above the ferns, adding to the already rather dense shade.

At one end of the path I have two camellias, 'Apollo' and 'Yours Truly', both of which do well. The 'Apollo' is very free flowering, the 'Yours Truly' has fewer flowers but is well worth having as they are a lovely veined pink with a narrow pure white edge. At the other end of the bed, cutting the whole thing off from the rest of the garden, is a gigantic clump of *Rosa* 'Canary Bird', so charming with its rows of tiny, single yellow flowers. There are also some delicate polygonum fighting their way up through the ferns. We have two species, *P. bistorta* 'Superbum' for spring and the tall, red *P. amplexicaule* for autumn. My other surprise plant for autumn is a disaster this year because of the lack of water. It is *Ligularia hodgsonii*. It has super great big leaves with purple backs and stems and then spires of orange-yellow daisy flowers in August. That is, in the past it had, this year it is a sad, lonely, drooping creature.

I nearly forgot. In the early spring there are two other things. A bank of Greek anemones, *Anemone blanda*, both white and blue. They carry on from the snowdrops, seeming to leap from the earth and then flower overnight the way an Amanita mushroom expands almost before your eyes in the summer woods. The second thing is a small clump of *Uvularia grandiflora*, the delicate relative of Solomon's Seal. To me, on this side of the Atlantic, it is rather rare and special, but as it's an American plant, you probably think of it as a weed.

Back to today. I have bulbs to order from my wholesaler. I

am planting a little, round bed in the middle of the garden for next spring – at present it is full of cosmos and sunflowers, surrounded by the common pink sedum. I am ordering: 1000 *Narcissi* 'Thalia', the orchid-flower narcissi, which will produce two or four flowers per head in early to mid April; 250 Greenland tulips; and 250 spring green tulips – these two from the 'Viridiflora' group, their green flowers edged with cream or old rose, will, I hope, make a subtle but fascinating combination. They should flower right after the narcissi, or so I hope. I am also ordering 1000 *Scilla bifolia* which are going to be planted in the grass amongst a little grove of the Himalayan birch, *Betula jacquemontii*. The scillas were at the request of an Old Etonian on the committee with a rather overbearing manner. He's called Oliver Baxter, a ball organizer by profession (balls as in dances), and when he isn't organizing he plagues me with some new plan or theory for the garden. Not that I mind, it keeps me on my toes. There is a super planting of scillas in Windsor Great Park near the Savill Garden. The Savill is one of the great gardens of southern England, with the most exciting collection of woodland plants I have ever seen. I have been making regular visits there to study the collection of rhododendrons – it includes many of the original plants collected by Forrest and other great plant collectors. Anyway, I digress. The reason I give the quantities of the bulbs is that the total cost amounts to only £187.50. At today's exchange rate that is $288. Although it's a lot of money it doesn't seem too bad for 2500 bulbs!

My arm is aching so I'm going to stop now. I hope you can read my scrawl.

Love,

Roger

SCALE 1mm ≈ 10cm (1/100)

BED 11: THE FERN BED

SHRUBS

A = *Aralia elata* 'Variegata'
B = *Azalea* 'Hino-mayo'
C = *Rhododendron* 'Alice'
D = *Camellia* 'Edwin H. Falk'
E = *Camellia* 'Adolphe Audusson'
F = *Camellia* 'Innovation'
G = *Camellia* 'Apollo' ×3
H = *Camellia* 'Yours Truly'
I = *Euonymus japonicus*
J = *Hedera helix*, common ivy

K = *Ilex aquifolium*, common holly
L = *Mahonia confusa*
M = *Mahonia japonicus*
N = *Platanus acerifolia*, the common London plane
O = *Prunus subhirtella* 'Autumnalis'
P = Rose 'Canary Bird'
Q = Rose 'Fragrant Cloud'
R = Rose 'Zephirine Drouhin'
S = *Viburnum tinus*

PERENNIALS

T = *Arum italicum*
U = *Athyrium filix-femina*, the Lady Fern
V = *Dicentra eximia* and *Dicentra spectabilis*
W = *Dryopteris filix-mas*, the Male Fern
X = *Epimedium alpinum*
Y = *Geranium endressii*
Z = *Hemerocallis flava*
AA = *Hosta sieboldiana*
AB = *Iris pseudocorus*, the wild yellow flag iris
AC = *Ligularia hodgsonii*
AD = *Petasites fragrans*, the winter heliotrope
AE = *Polygonum bistorta* 'Superbum'
AF = *Polygonum amplexicaule*
AG = *Onoclea sensibilis*, the American Oak Fern
AH = *Osmundia regalis*
AI = *Matteuccia struthiopteris*, the Shuttlecock Fern
AJ = *Scrophularia nodosa* 'Variegata', the variegated figwort
AK = *Symphytum caucasicum*, blue comfrey
AL = *Tolmiea menziesii*, the Pick-a-Back plant
AM = *Uvularia grandiflora*

Cushing, Maine

September 20 1989

Dear Roger,

I was delighted by your letter. Reply in kind shall be forthcoming, whenever I can find the time. Shortly off to New York for a week to see editors, etc, and before I go much work to do, not least of which is dealing with frost-probably-before-I-return. Plastic on the tomatoes, peppers, eggplants (aubergines) and shell beans. My shell beans this year are something called 'Bert Goodwin', reputedly a hundred-year-old family (not mine) heirloom from New Hampshire, and a nameless, big, white-seeded mystery bought last year at a grocery store in Hungary by my foody friend Nancy Jenkins.

Of course the *Acidanthera* are just starting – these things are sent to try us – but by and large it has been a good summer in spite of a ferocious drought. It's tempting to say conditions are not so different on our two sides of the Atlantic after all, but the truth is they really are. My garden is raw and new and carved out of something that could almost be called wilderness – at least it's wilderness compared to your venerable and unchangeable square in the heart (*is* it the heart?) of London.

I call the garden mine because I planned it and plant it, maintain and harvest it, but it actually belongs to Lois Dodd, a dear friend who has been kind enough to let me perch a little house (about which more some other time) on her property. There are five acres here, in a roughly triangular piece with one edge on the road. A deep gully with a stream at the bottom forms the other two sides, which meet at Lo's 'shore frontage', a ten-foot toehold on the bank of the Saint George river. I can see a sliver of silver and the neighbor's lobster

8

boat from my upstairs workroom, but that's about it for water views.

The old (well, roughly 1850s) farmhouse where Lois spends her summers has been my winter home since 1973, but until I came to live here year round I never did much work in the gardens because I had gardens of my own – ten miles down the road – that took all my time and attention. When I set up my summer studio here, at the other end of the land from the main house, I had to start again from scratch.

The place Lois bought in 1960 was a former sort-of-farm, potatoes the principal product, gone idle already for several decades. The entire hillside where my gardens are was badly overgrown with burdocks, roses, blackberries and seedling alders, birch, hawthorn and apple.

By the time I got ready to start *my* gardens, in 1980, this classic edge had become a scrub wood twenty to thirty feet tall, mostly full of popple (poplar) and alder, with an occasional baby oak and quite a few stripling birches (both paperbark and black birch) and tons of chokecherry (most of it full of black knot, which the remnants still sport). I had a backhoe come after everything but the birches and a group of apples at the edge of the lower garden had been chainsawed down. The earthmover removed most – though far from all – of the larger stumps, and a similar percentage of the bushel-basket-and-larger-size rocks.

So I started out with the gardens basically the same size they are now, only full of small-to-middle-size stumps and rocks of all sizes galore. Soil was and is extremely sandy, not as acid as might be feared (there's a lot of limestone nearby) but not what you'd call sweet, either.

Along the road, to the west and north, there is a narrow band, about thirty feet wide, of hackamatack (Eastern larch) and spruce, with an occasional white pine. These were already respectable trees when I came and now have achieved an authoritative height of 30 to 50 feet.

That's it for structure. Both upper and lower gardens are pretty much flat, because until three or four years ago I was sure I was about to move someplace more permanent. It seems so silly now, but I spent years refusing to plant even perennials, never mind shrubbery or trees, because I was afraid of losing them when I left. And now that I know I'm not moving and that in any case you can drag a lot of this material along? Well, every year I do plant more perennials, shrubs and trees, but I've gotten so involved with the ephemeral stuff there's scarcely room for anything else.

Or time, either, especially at this time of year, when the mushrooms take – or usually take – more than their share. This year's drought has been catastrophic though, for the mushrooms even more than the garden. We haven't had damn-all. Not even those straw-mulch-infesting, conical-capped, bright yellow deliquescers whose name temporarily escapes me, or the *Lepiota naucina* that usually infest the lawn in front of the upper garden. Have you had better luck? Of course, no mushrooms does leave more energy for tulip planting.

Being that boresome classic, an impoverished writer, I have to watch garden expenditures very closely. This has not kept me from ordering almost a hundred bucks' worth of spring bulbs. Generally gaudier choices than yours as my few scilla (sibirica) and 'Thalia' narcissi are almost lost in a host of the weirder sorts of tulips. Do you know the red parrot ones called 'Wonder'? I can't stay away from them. Immense flowers of great substance about the color of blood with greenish-maroon brushstrokes. They are not nice even a little and quite strong smelling with that peculiarly sexual, grassy, slightly-burnt smell of tulips. Great showerings of pollen, too, dark purple velvet fairy-dust courtesy a Tinkerbell from hell.

Thinking of bulbs leads me to ask what you do about hyacinths? Got to be one of the ugliest flowers in all creation no matter where you put them or what you do with them, but then there is that perfume, without which there is no spring. Are yours in England by any chance any better looking? (Can't see how they would be but in ignorance there is hope.) It has always seemed an enormous shame to me that the graceful little wood hyacinths have so little scent. In my garden, the big waddy Dutch ones are finally all right just before they give out. In the last two or three years the flowers are sort of mingy and attenuated, just an occasional bell here and there along the stem. Still a less than ideal arrangement but at least not such a sock in the eye, and the glorious fragrance persists undiminished. Can't help wishing there were an easier way, though . . .

And that I had more time to write. I'm looking forward to telling more, hearing more, all sorts of more, soon.

Leslie

28 September 1989

Dear Leslie,

I loved your letter.

One of the things our correspondence throws up is the plants that grow in one country and not in the other. You wrote about your *Acidanthera*, a plant I have never grown although I saw some in a lovely garden at Abbey Dore Court just a few days ago. Next spring I will order some and see if I can get them to bloom before winter.

This weekend I have been lionized at a mushroom weekend in the New Forest, the largest tract of preserved English woodland, 100,000 acres, untouched since Neolithic times. The epithet New was acquired in 1077 when William the Conquerer made it into his royal hunting preserve. The word 'forest' meant royal hunting wood, as opposed to 'chase' which means a hunting wood not owned by the king. Torres Spanish Wines invited top chefs from England and Paris for a mushroom banquet (Saturday night), mushroom foray with me as guide and identifier (Sunday morning), *gran paella* in the woods (Sunday lunch). The lunch was sublime – the paella pan was over three feet across. The dish was black rice – *arroz negro*. José Puig (pronounced putch), the European sales manager organized the whole thing for publicity. Apart from being a wine expert he has two other overriding interests, wild mushrooms and cooking *al fresco*. He did the cooking. The cuttlefish ink and the pan had both been carted over from Spain. Building the fire was my contribution – no paper and only one match – this is my one and only party piece. José went away a very happy man. From memory here's how it was done:

3 lb onions

10 sweet red peppers

3 cloves garlic

all chopped fried in 2 pints of real olive oil (slowly). Then add 6 lbs of chopped squid (half-inch cubes) and cook slowly for 20 minutes, then 6 lbs rice and stir for 3 minutes, then most of 12 pints of fish stock, the rest added as it cooks. Then the important thing, the magic touch, the ink from the squid which instantly turns the rice black. The result got a standing ovation! It is a primitive fisherman's dish eaten when times were bad: I suspect if times were really bad they would sell the squid and make it with only the ink! It comes from the district on the Spanish coast between Tarragona and Alicante, where Spanish rice is grown.

Back to the garden. Yes, Eccleston Square is right in the centre of London, in Pimlico, roughly the area between the Thames, the Houses of Parliament, Buckingham Palace and Chelsea.

Many garden squares are neglected, usually the fault of the old dodderers on the garden committees. (There are 461 squares in London – or were at the last survey.) What happens is that the big trees keep going, taking all the water from the soil which gradually ends up a dry powder. For the first couple of years I spent about half my time mulching with peat, with spent hops from our local brewery, with bark mulch and finally with our own leaf mould.

We are allowed to use the hoses again now. The ban has been lifted after six weeks so I am trying to bring back to life the sad, weakened, unhappy plants. The azaleas, rhododendrons, pieris and hydrangeas have fared worst – five or six have had it – but the camellias have gone through with hardly a leaf lost. They are ten times as drought tolerant as I had thought.

We have a new quality Sunday newspaper in Britain, the

Correspondent. The gardening column is written by Victoria Glendinning, who is a biographer. She kicked off her column by talking about the thick skin on the soles of her feet from going barefoot all summer and how she picked it off with her nails and ate it. Perhaps my way of telling you about the garden and my thoughts is too mundane! Tell me something about you – what happened to your husband, what caused you to go it alone? . . .

10 October

Since I started this letter all *hell* has broken loose. At ten to eleven on Friday night, 29 September, I had a gardener's nightmare. The telephone rang and a Professor Lovejoy, who represents the company who own the freehold of the square garden, told me that they have a plan to dig up the whole three acres and put in a three-storey nine-hundred-car underground car park – afterwards covering it up again, ostensibly as we wished. I spent the whole night pacing up and down planning and plotting every form of objection and action right up to and including murder. Churchill lived in the square at the turn of the century and we are going to use his drawing room for the meetings of our war cabinet.

Life is too chaotic to say more – I will write again soon with more garden talk.

Love,

Roger

P.S. At the weekend I went out mushrooming and found four perfect condition giant puffballs. I made an ordinary batter and cut two in slices and dunked them in it, then fried them in shallow oil in a frying pan. After one side was nicely brown I turned them and sprinkled grated Cheddar cheese on top. By the time the underside had cooked the cheese on top had melted. The whole thing was mouth-wateringly good.

Cushing, Maine

October 19 1989

Just got your letter OmiGod what appalling news. May it turn out to be a threat and nothing more. I'll write very soon at greater length but wanted you to know I'm thinking of you and your garden (and the wickedness of the world) very nearly nonstop.

Leslie

Cushing, Maine

October 22 1989

Good grief Roger how can the man's name be Professor Lovejoy and where is Nabokov when we need him? I keep having this fantasy that the whole thing is some awful dream, or a scam you have thought up to give your letters a bit of potboilerish pizzaz. But I suppose it's all too true: this kind of shortsighted idiocy usually is. Any chance of help from official agencies? There sure as hell wouldn't be here, but we do have a brand new private organization set up – I think – to deal with just this sort of thing. Actually, I have a feeling they're more worried about neglect-at-death-or-financial-reversal-of-owner, but they might be able to suggest something or at least give you some US publicity. It's The Garden Conservancy, Box 219 Main Street, Cold Spring, N.Y., and the contact would be Frank Cabot, a major American garden honcho whom I've never met but recently had a nice phone chat with as I may be writing up his white garden for a magazine piece. Your name is likely to be more useful than mine (I don't know if he'd even remember me, though we talked for quite a while) but feel free, etc. . .

Your woes do put mine into perspective. Somehow Nature's blows are easier to support, even when they get help from humankind. It *did* frost in my absence, and my helper, who is game but inexperienced, didn't recognize the warning signs, as a result of which much produce and annual floriferation was lost that needn't have been. In fact it's probably just as well as I'm too busy to do much putting-up, cooking or even eating if it requires more than washing something off. Still out there plugging along are the usual hardy vegetables: lettuces, carrots, beets, leeks and the like. Perhaps I should mention here, *à la* Glendinning, that although I adore braised leeks and cook them frequently (usually in butter, with browned shreds of lime zest and the lime juice), they make me fart like a bandit and I can only enjoy them when I expect a full day of solitude in which to toot unabashed.

Of flowers there is little left – Korean chrysanthemums, which every few years I spend major energy extirpating root and branch and then I realize nothing else blooms so late, so reliably and I go find some tiny escapee of my wrath and encourage it and by the next year they are again the rampant weed I can't bear and the whole drama starts again. Also still at it are the white California poppies (*Eschscholzia californicum*), possibly my favorite plant. In spite of their name they do splendidly here, reseeding so reliably as to be perennials for all practical purposes. They are the first flowers of spring as well as the last of fall, their feathery grey-blue foliage and pale cream-primrose-fading-to-white flowers welcome in every situation. Most sources I've read describe them as low and matlike in habit, but here they top out at about eighteen inches and spread just about as far as you'll let them – lots of graceful arching and Japanese attitudes. And they're dandy cut, too – last forever and you don't even have to burn the ends. Obligingly, the roots are shallowish and they don't seem to compete with the things they're right smack on top of – I let 'em go under the roses in the white garden and they get all tangled with the equally-obliging alyssum (a plant I adore in spite of its unhappily plebeian associations). *Calendula* of course still hanging in. Do you know the variety 'Touch of Red'? It has strokes of dark brick-rust color up the backs of the petals that makes the orange ones especially glow like neon (much better than the 'Neon' variety which, at least in my garden, produces small flowers that refuse to open flat in the correct calendulesque way although, credit where credit is due, even the partially-expanded buds of 'Neon' are pretty spectacular). And of course there are pansies. Most of the pansies are in the blue border, ribbons of varieties called 'True Blue' and 'Black Devil', as well as assorted sports of the latter. Would that there were other flowers as black as the blackest of these, but that deep, velvety, light-sucking *true* black is unique in my experience.

Needless to say, I no sooner sent my drought-complaint letter than it commenced to rain . . . and rain . . . and rain. Where no mushrooms were there is now abundance, so I have to switch my complaint to one about having no time to go and pick. The people down the road who always call me when the horse mushrooms (*Agaricus arvensis*) start on their lawn called again to say something strange was spreading in the sheep-manured strip by the edge of their woods. Bingo! *Lepista* (*Tricholoma, Clitocybe,* when did *you* learn to call their name?) either *saeva* or *irina,* the not-blue blewits in any event, in good numbers and grand condition and, eventually, soup. There's still about a pound of them in the fridge awaiting – little time to cook and no one to share them with. My easy to be with sans social production nearby good friends, an otherwise sensible couple, don't like mushrooms.

What I eventually did was to cook the last lepistas and

horse mushrooms together with onion in butter and then braise them in some ancient duck stock I found lurking in the freezer. This I made into some assorted sauces. The best: reduce the whole thing to a paste, add cream and reduce again, then pour the intense charcoal-grey mess over a pile of steamed cauliflower and shower lightly with grated Parmesan. It turned out quite handsomely black and white and although no one saw I found the hardship endurable as I was thus able to pig down the whole thing by myself.

Driving to town I see troops of shaggy manes taking over the front yards. The woods called madly just yesterday, the first dry day though it was blowing a gale, so I went – telling myself it would probably be the last time because once the hunting season starts (next Sat.) the price is way too high. Some hunters here are most cavalier and 'blaze orange' clothing is no protection against fools who know there's little chance of trouble even if they do screw up. Last year a woman was shot and killed in her own backyard, less than two hundred yards from her door. And the grand jury didn't even indict for manslaughter. She was a stranger 'from away' and the man who shot her – he insists he had a deer in his sights at the time though no sign of one was found – was a local fellow, scout leader and all around good guy. General opinion seems to have been that it was her own fault because she wasn't wearing any orange and she had on white mittens, which might have been mistaken for the nether end of a white-tailed deer. Everyone knows that's the wrong end to shoot even if it *is* a deer but that seems to have carried no weight. Neither did the fact that the hunter was illegally too close to a house – the victim's neighbor's house – when the shooting took place.

Life in the country. I love it. Especially when it's not hunting season. (In the still safe woods I found rather a lot of inedible *Cortinarii*, not very many almond and pine *Hygrophori* and a whole charge of something that's almost *Tricholoma portentosum* but not quite I don't think. No help from my admittedly small collection of the usual guides – Gary's, David Arora's, and an Italian item by Rinaldi and Tyndalo called (sigh) *The Complete Book of Mushrooms* that's actually the best of the lot as far as the pics go. The illustrations are water color and – no offense, but – as far as I'm concerned paintings beat photos going away for ID purposes. I shall document it, take a photo with my inadequate polaroid and maybe dry a couple for later identification from someone who, unlike me, knows something.

The mystery items came from the mostly oak-canopied spot by the river where I lived in the summer before I came here year round. It was a very special place, a fairytale cottage down a dirt lane a third of a mile from the main road, fully equipped with splendid views, electricity and phone, no running water (pump in the yard), lots of eccentric architectural embellishment from the hand of the sculptor whose cottage it had been for decades. It finally biodegraded and had to be torn down. The cellarhole and burnt ruins of the studio (the owner gave the place to the fire department to practice on) are still there, as are the lilies of the valley in spring and the mushrooms in the fall.

My former main garden (a roughly thirty- by one-hundred-foot rectangle plowed out of the sloping field just up the hill on the other side of an alder brake) has gone back totally, though the three-foot-deep drainage ditch I dug (by hand, ain't youth wonderful) all round the perimeter has remained, a trap for the unwary. I'd built a tiny thyme garden by the path to the river and that lasted longer than anything else but I thought this time it was finally gone. After all, it's been nine years. There was no sign that I could see of anything but mosses and lichens – the spruce next to it is tall now – assorted expected weeds, bare patches. The soil is pure clay. I stepped right into it to look more closely and saw nothing, felt a sighing sadness, then caught the fragrance of thyme triumphant, bruised but not crushed underfoot. It really is tough stuff. Won't be long now, though, I expect, and all else is so much changed I don't know that I won't be glad when my last traces are erased. What will I hunt then when I walk in those woods?

An academic question, actually, as development is fast encroaching and those woods are unlikely to remain for many more years. They are already much diminished from when I first knew them.

October 29

No time now to go on as it's gorgeous out: sunny and seventy degrees, 'unseasonably warm' with bells on. It's probably global warming or the end of the world or something but it's such a novelty to be cleaning up the garden, planting the bulbs, etc. in a tee-shirt that even the mosquito bites (!) are a small price to pay.

Best love,
Leslie

P.S. This is from a recent column – thought it might give you an idea or two.

EAST–WEST MUSHROOM SOUP WITH
MUSHROOM DUMPLINGS

for 6 servings:

1½ tablespoons butter
1 tablespoon olive oil
2 cups chopped onion, 1 very large or 2 medium
1 lb firm mushrooms, wild ones such as horse mushrooms or

king boletes or blewits, or 12 oz commercial mushrooms
mixed with 4 oz shiitakes
1 large clove garlic, quartered
1 small carrot, chopped fine
6 cups (2½ pints) water
1 egg white
¼ lb ground pork
a heaping teaspoon fresh ginger, shredded on the fine holes of
the grater
1 large garlic clove, minced fine
1 teaspoon soy sauce
36 fresh wonton wrappers
2 tablespoons marsala or medium-sweet madeira
salt to taste
2 tablespoons snipped chives

Combine butter and olive oil in a large saucepan over
medium heat. When the butter melts, add the onion, turn the
heat to low and cook *very slowly* until the onion is dark
golden and caramelized. This may take as long as 45 minutes
but little stirring is required until close to the end.

Save one or two of the firmest mushroom caps to slice for
the garnish later and chop the rest into roughly ⅓ inch dice.
When the onions are ready, add the mushrooms, raise the
heat to medium high and cook, stirring, until the mushrooms
have lost their liquid and begun to brown. This will take
anywhere from four or five to ten or twelve minutes,
depending on the moistness of the material.

The pile of mushrooms will seem enormous at the start,
and it may smell a bit odd during the cooking down part. But
the quantity will reduce enormously and the funny fragrance
– if there is one – will quickly vanish.

Once the mushrooms have started to brown you'll soon
have something that looks like rich, lumpy paste. Remove
and reserve a scant ⅔ cup of it. Add the garlic and carrot to

what remains in the pan, pour in the water, cover and simmer over very low heat for an hour or a little more.

Strain the soup, pressing to get all the flavorful juice, then discard the solids. Return the liquid to the wiped-out pan.

Meanwhile, as soon as the reserved mushroom mixture has cooled off, combine it with the egg white, pork, ginger, garlic and soy. Set out wrappers on the work surface and put a teaspoon-sized dollop of the filling on each one. Dampen the edges with cold water, then fold into triangles and seal. Press the long ends together in the center and set the finished dumplings aside.

Bring a large kettle/pot of salted water to boil when the soup is almost cooked. Gently drop in the prepared dumplings and cook for 5 minutes, or until they are swollen and appear to be almost done. Strain the soup while they are cooking. The idea is to transfer the dumplings directly, using a slotted spoon, from the boiling water to the soup where they should finish cooking in another 5 minutes or so. Stir in the wine and salt to taste.

Slice the reserved mushroom caps quite thinly and set aside. When the soup is ready, divide it among the bowls and float a few slices of mushroom in each. Sprinkle with chives and serve at once.

ECCLESTON SQUARE,
LONDON

8 November 1989

Dear Leslie,

Thanks for your letter full of support and ideas. I have formed a Society for the Protection of London Squares and I am busy (apart from producing three or four books) contacting other squares and gardens to gather together an unstoppable landslide of garden lovers to overwhelm our city planners and the awful Lovejoy and his masters.

When I think about it you probably have no real idea of what our square looks like – so here goes with a plan, so you can follow what I drone on about.

ECCLESTON SQUARE BED PLAN

Notes on the most interesting beds and plants

Bed 1 Is kept by Beryl Pye who is a terrific woman devoted to
gardening. She keeps up the whole area, probably the
equivalent of a normal back garden, buying
everything for it and planting
out to make it her own
cottage garden.

Bed 2 Is our herb garden. It is actually a series of tiny beds about one pace square, each planted with different herbs.

Bed 3 Is a small rather shady area which is looked after by Dierdre Pratt, who goes to a great deal of trouble to keep it going.

Bed 5 The main ceanothus bed, although there are loads more ceanothus dotted around the garden.

Bed 6 The main camellia collection.

Bed 7 Is underplanted with a collection of Dog-Toothed Violets.

Bed 10 Arthur the gardener has created a delightful scree garden here.

Bed 11 The fern garden: this whole area is kept rather damp, and wild irises and other damp-loving things flourish here.

Bed 12 Is our old rose collection.

Bed 13 Is kept, designed, gardened or whatever, by Di and John Goulden who are busily turning it into a collection of interesting variegated shrubs.

Bed 14 Is our winter garden mainly planted with hellebores but also with a few early flowering comfreys.

Bed 15 Has a small collection of flowering cherries and lots of hydrangeas.

Bed 16 Has lots of shrub roses including big Nevada and Marguerite Hilling.

Bed 17 Here a great bank of *Viburnum plicatum Mariesii* is backed by lovely clumps of swaying bamboo.

Bed 22 Is a collection of mainly deciduous azaleas, especially varieties of Exbury azaleas which do by far the best in our rather neutral soil. They are mixed with and given some shade by four or five different Japanese maples.

Bed 23 An evergreen magnolia is underplanted with tulips which are followed by ground-cover roses.

Bed 24 Features a tulip tree underplanted with a mixture of lavender and ground-cover ceanothus.

Bed 25 The yellow bed which has yellow-leaved shrubs and predominantly, though not exclusively, yellow flowers.

Bed 26 Climbing roses underplanted with day lilies.

Bed 27 Climbing roses are underplanted with Tall Bearded Irises.

Bed 30 Old roses, especially Chinas.

Bed 31 Annuals and perennials.

Beds 33/34 The main planting is peonies.

Bed 39 A massive planting of some 200 different irises.

A few of the more exceptional plants have been sketched in to give you an idea of their size and position.

A = *Parrotia persica* the Persian Ironwood Tree. A wonderful mixture of autumn colours.

B = *Exochorda* 'The Bride'. A lovely pendulous shape with the white blossom veiling it as a bride in the early spring.

C = *Callistemon citrinus*, the Bottlebrush. In July it is a delight just bordering on the patio where we have 'barbies'. Very appropriate.

D = *Paulownia tomentosa*, the Foxglove Tree. This will be its fourth season and I hope it will make it into flower for the first time.

E = *Clianthus puniceus*, the Kaka Beak shrub from New Zealand. Its common name comes from the Kaka bird which has a vicious hooked beak for tearing flesh.

F = *Senecio rotundifolia*, the Muttonbird shrub. This shrub, also from New Zealand, is supposed to be tender but it has survived a couple of harsh winters without any problems. Its botanical name has now changed to *Brachyglottis rotundifolia*.

G = *Liquidamber styraciflua* 'Worplesdon'. This is the form of Sweetgum that gives the best autumn colour.

H = Three Japanese maples in a loose group.

I = *Rose filipes* 'Kiftsgate'. As far as I know this is the biggest growing rose you can get. Anyway, I am trying – with some success – to grow it up one of our giant London Planes.

J = *Prunus mume*, the little Japanese Shrub Almond. This is one of the five principal plants of Japanese gardens because of its stalwart ability to fight its way into flower in the snow at the end of January. It is superbly scented too.

K = *Pittosporum tobira*, from China and the east. Again this is thought to be a tender thing but frost has caused it no damage and the scent is terrific in April.

L = *Crinodendron hookeranum* from Chile. Its flowers are lovely little red lanterns.

M = *Betula jacquemontii*. A group of five Himalayan Birch. It has super peeling pinkish bark.

N = *Davidea involucrata*, the Handkerchief Tree.

O = *Morus nigra*, the Black Mulberry, was planted by Colin Lowry who has been on the garden committee for yonks. It is a cutting from a very ancient plant from his parents' garden. Mullberries are one of my all-time favourite fruits although beating the birds to it is a task and a half.

P = *Corylopsis sinensis*, delicate catkins, in March.

Q = A group of deciduous magnolias.

R = A fine specimen of *Liquidamber styraciflua*, the Sweetgum.

S = *Callicarpa bodinieri* variety *giraldii*. This has masses of violet berries all through the winter.

Last week I went up to Nottinghamshire to visit a very grand country house at Flintham which had wonderful walled gardens and parkland (not to mention a giant conservatory). David who took me round (in the company of Elizabeth Luard, a fine cookery writer), ended up by giving me a box of medlars and a box of quinces. How did these garden marvels ever fall from grace? I now am desperate to get both for the garden.

The medlar *Mespilus germanica* makes a lovely specimen tree turning a superb golden sunset colour in the autumn. When I was a child I was told the word medlar meant 'open arsehole' in Anglo-Saxon! Presumably from the appearance of the fruit 'with its broad open eye, surrounded by the persistent calyx . . .' (Bean). Anyway they are picked at the end of October and allowed to start to decay – 'bletted'. I just boiled them up in sufficient water to cover them, for one hour, until they had turned to a pulp, then I strained the mush through an old baby's cloth nappy and added 1 lb of sugar to each pint of liquid, simmered this until it started to set on the saucer and then bottled it. It is a little low on pectin I think and it benefits from the addition of a few sour apples, but whichever way it is a great concoction.

The quinces, *Cydonia oblonga*, I chopped up and boiled for about forty minutes, just floating in water, then strained it through the nappy. Again 1 lb of sugar to a pint of the liquid reduced to setting point, makes a fantastic jelly with a lovely clear pinky cerise-red colour. And then you put the mush in a saucepan with a little of the liquid (1 lb of sugar to 1 lb of mush), simmer for twenty minutes, making sure it doesn't catch – then you pot it up. A great jam with the texture of a thick marmalade is the result. All my friends have gone wild for all three concoctions and almost all has already been eaten.

Now I begin my search for the plants. Quince by the way has wonderfully scented flowers and also good autumn colour. Hillier's, our great tree and shrub people, have in their manual a special fruit tree list with named cultivars of both – presumably with large fruit, good colour, reliable quantities, etc. Half an hour later after phoning round I have raised both *Mespilus germanica*, a form called 'Nottingham', which apparently has the best-flavoured fruit, and *Cydonia oblonga* 'Portugal', large fruit, light orange in colour.

Incidentally, your leek story reminded me of a biography I read years ago of one of the Sioux chiefs who said that when they started to eat and drink the food of the white Americans their 'air' became bad. This suggests two things to me: a) farting was not a taboo subject, and b) a very natural diet doesn't cause such a pong!

Some 'trendy' did a series on TV called *Mushroom Magic* in England this autumn, and it proved very popular. I had nothing to do with making it, but the people who did said that wherever they went my name cropped up – i.e. in France, when the French collectors found a mushroom they couldn't identify, the cry would go up *'prendre Le Phillips'* and my book would be dragged out to help. Anyway they rang my publishers and, having ascertained that I was not dead, they came and filmed me in my room just rabbiting on about mushrooms. They then hacked up the film and put a few minutes in each of the six half-hour programmes.

The result has been that my Mushroom book sales have

rocketed: October 1988 sales 252, October 1989 sales 2,004! All of which leads me to believe that the only way for the likes of us to make any real cash is to get on telly. So I have been chatting to TV production companies and as I know nothing about that world I have now got myself an agent.

Leslie, your Californian poppy is a revelation. Having seen it beside the roads right across Arizona I presumed it would be useless in my garden in London. Thompson & Morgan have seeds of eight different cultivated forms only one of which is white – *Eschscholzia caespitosa* 'Milky White'. I hope this is your one. Anyway I have ordered seed and some of the other colour forms as well, I shall put most of the seed out on to the beds when I get it and see if I can get a late natural germination. My cosmos has seeded all over the gravel path but I expect they will all be killed when the temperature drops. I can only hope.

10 November

The cold weather continues. I am thinking of ways to protect my tender plants if we start to get temperatures of below −5°C (24°F). I expect this is a nightly occurrence for you.

Love,

Roger

Cushing, Maine

Roger my peach,

What a lovely present. (Book on white gardens.) How kind of you to think of me . . . and in the midst of such troubles, too. How goes the good fight? I keep trying to track down a song for you that might be helpful in the campaign. It's called (I think) 'Big Yellow Taxi'. It's by Joni Mitchell, and the refrain is 'You don't know what you've got till it's gone – they paved paradise and put up a parking lot.'

I'm frantically busy but will write soon – I kiss you and feed you mushrooms & say thanks so very kindly much again.

L

Cushing, Maine

Dear Roger,

Do forgive me for being so long in writing and no excuse really except a severe attack of Life.

Plus the weather has been inconvenient in the extreme – giant snowstorm on November 21, the earliest in my experience here. Followed, not as usually happens even in December and January by rain, but instead by ongoing record cold – it's 6°F as I write this (10 pm) and supposed to get colder as the (endless, I long for solstice) night wears on. Mercifully the one day of rain and above freezing temperature we had last week was not enough to completely melt the snowcover and I can only hope it'll be enough to protect the brand newly planted peonies. I finally sprang for four: 'Elsa Sass', 'Florence Nicholls', 'Nancy Nicholls' and 'Ray Payton' – two whites, one pink and one red – all of them set in the ground a bare week before the storm and of course I had the *best* intentions of mulching them but . . . The roses thank heaven were already earthed up around the crowns, but I have not yet wrapped the protruding canes with reemay (spun polyester, do you know about/ use it?) as I intend to do it for an experiment. Each year except for the rugosas my roses die back almost to where the earthing ends, even the floribundas and the hybrid perpetuals which shouldn't do any such thing. So this year I drove stake cages around each plant, intending to fill them with leaves and wrap same with reemay. Leaves at this point clearly out but I may yet get to the wrapping and perhaps do the stuffing with straw if I can find some to buy.

Not all the bulbs had gone in pre-storm either, but I went out the other day and scraped aside the snow and sure enough underneath it was still diggable if not exactly toasty so I've

buried the stragglers quite deep with lots of lovely bonemeal
and will hope for the best.

At least the snow is beautiful. It's always such a relief to see
the landscape smoothed out, simplified, made whole. Went
skiing over last weekend and found the woods very calm and
harmonious in their white cladding. Spiders evidently as
surprised by the weather as the rest of us: their webs were still
everywhere – little silken laundry lines with perfect snow-
flakes hung out in rows to dry.

Interesting about your new/ old fruits. According to the
excellent *Fruit, Nut and Berry Inventory* put out by our Seed
Savers Exchange, medlars are 'botanically somewhere
between a pear and a hawthorn'. The former do okay here,
though it seems to be the northern end of possibility for them
and fire blight is a problem. Hawthorn thrives (I live on a spit
of land called Hawthorne Point and though that's for a person
– distant relative of Nathaniel – it might as well be for the
tree). Five different medlars are available, though only two –
the species and 'Nottingham' (guess it really must be the best)
are described. Of quinces we can get quite a lot; the *Inventory*
lists eight, but none of them are your 'Portugal'. Portugal *is*
named as a parent (along with Orange, a 'very old variety') of
something called 'Van Deman', introduced in 1891, hybrid-
ized by – who else? – Luther Burbank.

Quinces I know do grow in these parts. My friend Carol
Lundquist has access to a tree, makes jelly that sounds like
yours except that it's more apricot/carnelian color; and years
ago I came across a fine old large tree some little distance
from an abandoned road in the woods where I had gone to
look for mushrooms. I filled my jacket with the fruits, which
were completely sound and quite plump in spite of their
comparatively sunless situation, but foolishly failed to take
sufficiently careful notice of the spot. I've never found it
again.

Some earlier inhabitant must have planted that quince,

they don't grow wild here. I didn't search for more evidence at the time but I usually do. There's something about these obscure vignettes of former lives that's very powerful. Our woods are full of old cellar holes, tumbled-down chimneys, ancient scraggly lilacs absurdly tall still stretching towards the light. Cushing, for instance, though it's now close to entirely tree-clad was cleared bald as the proverbial egg a century ago. All those farms have grown over and gone; their farmers fled West to land that brings forth something other than rocks.

Only we gardeners persist, plus our one farmer – Gerald Smith – who grows sweet corn and squash on exquisite land overlooking the river. He'd have lost the place long ago were it not that Maine has an easement system whereby agricultural land can be exempted from being taxed at its full development value. His son David is a farmer too, but does not live on or seem to have hope of inheriting his father's place (too many kids?). David was in dairying until the big 'whole herd buyout' of three or four years ago and he now grows hay, hauls gravel and makes do. Still young (I think in his early thirties) he'll probably move to upstate New York, where land is still cheap enough (and good enough) to permit dairy farming. So the story continues to repeat itself.

I won't go on at length about the unfortunate effect of onions, but do want to say that your Sioux chief's observations are suggestive of what I know about the problems encountered by those unfortunates who, convinced by the health and morality pundits, suddenly begin eating lots of dried beans. It should be a gradual process; you have to slowly build up your population of the appropriate intestinal flora (and presumably, fauna), the ones that digest the unaccustomed saccharides before the ill-wind situation begins to correct itself. Soaking the legumes overnight and then throwing out the soaking water is also efficacious but you probably already know that.

Haven't been cooking much lately myself, too busy with

34

both work and chores: another storm has meant much hauling of firewood, shovelling of snow, etc., leading me to reflect that whoever said 'all a woman needs to be happy is a cat and a cucumber' sure as hell didn't live in the country. But I did make a nice duck with wild mushrooms at Thanksgiving time.

DOUBLE DUCK (STEWED AND GRILLED) WITH WILD MUSHROOMS

Carve the breasts from a four-pound domestic duck and set aside in the fridge. Skin and joint the rest of the bird and refrigerate legs, thighs and meaty sections. (Render out the fat and cracklings for other uses i.e. gingerbread, the fat makes great gingerbread).

Put the carcass, neck and outer wing pieces in a shallow pan with an onion (trimmed but unpeeled) and a few chunks of carrot and roast hot until well browned. Break everything up, cover generously with hot water (use same to deglaze roasting pan) and make strong stock, aiming to end up with about three cups (1½ pints) of fairly fat-free broth (omit usual aromatics).

Brown the legs, thighs, giblets and heart in a bit of the duck fat, add *a lot* of dried boletes (about two lightly piled cups of pieces, a couple of ounces) and the broth. Cook until the meat falls apart, by which time the mushrooms will be thoroughly cooked and there will be only enough broth left to be a sauce. Season very lightly as needed – I used only a pinch of salt and about one tablespoon of port.

Score the skin of the duck breasts crosshatch and broil/grill about six minutes without turning to get crisp skin and rare meat. Slice breasts across the grain and arrange in the center of a shallow serving dish surrounded by the stew. I served it with boiled potatoes at least partly because I wanted to show off my all-blues (they're a lovely lavender clear through when cooked and have a special, slightly smoky taste that I think is more than psychological) but I can't think of *any* saucemop that wouldn't suit. Wild mushroom pasta would be especially nice. Can you get it there? We have a tasty brand of dried, Gaston Dupre, and some speciality stores – not here, of course – sell it fresh.

World Going To Hell in a Handbasket Department: can you believe my duck didn't have a liver (rare bird indeed). What it had, to my great disgust, was an obscenely large, very squidgy packet of 'Orange Sauce' full, according to the label, of sugar, additives and orange flavoring. Directions advised heating this up and then sloshing it over the poor creature after it had been roasted for about three and a half years (or until the plastic thingummy it had been impaled with popped up) by which point it would undoubtedly need all the help it could get. Phooey.

Enclosed find a copy of the song I mentioned. Joni Mitchell is big for good causes so I'm sure would give permission if there was any way to use that oh so appropriate refrain in the fight to save the garden.

Work calls,

Leslie

P.S. I'm sure my California Poppy is *E. californicum*. *E. caespitosa* is supposed to be fragrant, which mine ain't, and very short, ditto.

Eccleston Square,
London

20 December 1989

Dear Leslie,

I am horrified at the temperatures in Cushing. It at last brings home to me why gardens in America are so different from ours. (Our low has been about 22°F in London so far this year.)

I tend to think of a garden as a collection of shrubs; the perennials provide low cover and some summer flowers but really only augment the shrubs. I think of *Choisya*, Mexican Orange Blossom, as a quick-growing, dark background evergreen with lovely scented leaves and flowers which come out at any old time of year (often twice) but now your letter has brought home to me that you could never grow it. The other thing that I cannot get through my thick head is that you are over five hundred miles south of me – by my map you come out on the same latitude as the French Rivieras, and to boot you are near the sea. How can it be so cold? In England, anywhere around the coast, you really don't get frost at all yet we are on a latitude that runs just north of Newfoundland. All this is down to the Gulf Stream, otherwise we would not even be able to survive here never mind garden.

For the moment we have seen off the car park plan. The developers have shown us their weakness – they hate publicity. The *Daily Telegraph* did a big article on the story taking them to task for their thoughtless greed. Shortly afterwards the developers sent me a letter confirming that they were not planning to proceed with the car park.

We have won the battle but not the war. That will no doubt creep up on us in a much more underhand manner sometime in the future. One of my ideas for future publicity if it is needed is to stand on the steps of Churchill's house and do the 'V for victory' sign for the camera. My main line for future resistance is our Society for the Protection of London Squares. As soon as any developer sticks his neck out we will bury an axe in it with the combined force of perhaps four hundred squares (100,000 residents).

As we are a conservation area our trees are automatically preserved with a TPO (Tree Protection Order) on each but, as I suspected, the council tree maps were extremely out of date. So I got the council tree man round and we mapped every single tree in the square down to the very smallest. This means that any future horrible desecrators would have to overturn in the region of forty TPOs to do their dirty digging.

Reemay sounds interesting. I have been starting to put in rather tender things over the last two years as we really haven't had a winter. This year I have cut long bamboos and made wigwam frames over the tender shrubs. Then when the weather gets cold I wrap clear plastic over them and staple it on, the thought being that light can get through whilst affording some protection from the cold and especially the cold wind. But it looks dreadful.

My mimosa, *Acacia baileyana*, is about ten feet tall and dropping with flower buds. I hope they will open in January but maybe I will have to wait until April. It is much too tall to build a wigwam over so I have just given it a roof over its head; my latest theory is that this will give it a 5 to 10°F advantage over an open-grown plant.

Do mahonias survive in your temperature? My *Mahonia* × *media* 'Charity' is in full flower and has been for about a month with still three or four weeks to go. Although the leaves are barbarously prickly it is wonderful to cut a piece and bring it into the house, the scent of the sweet smelling yellow flowers pervades every corner. Another plant I grow that is just coming into flower is the perennial weed *Petasites fragrans*, winter heliotrope, which flowers all through January and has a delicious marzipan scent. It probably would grow in your garden but perhaps it would be best not to try as it propagates itself at an amazing rate through its underground shoots which even when they hit a wall will go down a foot or two to get beyond it. My soil is a black friable loam and

Flowers December—
January scented
like marzipan

The leaves come
as the flowers die

Petasites fragrans
Winter Heliotrope

when it spreads too far I can just spend ten minutes pulling it out to keep it under control. Friends who have clay soil never get rid of it and cannot believe that I persist with it.

By the way 'Big Yellow Taxi' by Joni Mitchell is definitely my theme song from now on. She's certainly got her finger on the desecration pulse.

> Took all the trees and put them in a tree museum,
> And they charged all the people a dollar and a half
>   just to see them.
> They paved paradise and put up a parking lot,
> With a pink hotel, a boutique and a swinging hot-
>   spot,
> Don't it always seem to go
> That you don't know what you've got till it's gone.

3 January 1990

I can't continue without first mentioning eastern Europe. The changes have been so vast and yet so quick that we all have ended up not knowing which way is up. Romania was inspiring, seeing the students taunting the security police to shoot at them so that the army could locate and then ferret them out. Literally using their lives as bait. A Romanian expatriate on English radio asked people to burn candles in their windows to support and commemorate them. We did and I hope every Christmas to make it a special feature to remind us all of their bravery and sacrifice.

A super surprise in the garden. Last year Martyn Rix, who

Tuber
life size

cream
with dashes
of bright red

is a great bulb expert, gave me a couple of tubers of
Tropaeolum tuberosum. I planted them under some large dark
Euonymus japonica shrubs and they rapidly ran right up
through the shrubs and then burst into flower in midsummer
and didn't stop until November – little red and yellow trumpets like a narrow flowered aquilegia – a real joy, especially
for the late season. But this is not what surprised me; when I
went to dig them up for the winter I discovered that each of
the tubers now had progeny – thirty or forty new tubers! If
that is not propagation it's certainly multiplication. The garden next autumn will be draped in the things and will look
like some wonderful Andean mountain in Peru. The year
after?

Love,

Roger

Cushing, Maine

Dear Roger,

It's snowing, about 11 degrees, inconvenient in some ways but in others a great relief. We needed snow. The January thaw (we do always get one) arrived in the rain on New Year's Eve and has proceeded intermittently ever since, so by this week most of the old snow cover had melted off. Poor ol' plants were naked (and getting heaved) and the landscape was ugly you bet, a dispiriting wasteland of dirty old snow, mottled ice, and mud dotted here and there with three months' worth of the beer bottles and fast food wrappers our local punks casually discard from the windows of their cars.

This has actually been a much snowier year than usual. Being on the coast we're much more likely to get sleet, freezing rain and just plain cold. I'll be very interested to see what spring brings since the surprise snow of last fall meant I put on a lot less winter protection than usual. Can't wait to see who survives and who don't and whether the perennially failing but never quite dying tree peony makes it through. It's Lois's, so I can't quite wish its demise, but the damned thing is such a tease – it never gets more than about eighteen inches tall and always has one flower bud, which blasts, that I can't quite wish it a long life either.

The Christmas camellias you told me about on the phone live in my head (the only thing blooming here is the heliotrope in the sunroom, flowering its fool head off and smelling like grandmother). Also alive in my head is your request to hear about the Christmas tree so here it is. Please bear in mind that Christmasness is already half-faded from memory, the object itself now whacked up into boughs and covering the bed of *Fragaria moschata* at the edge of the upper garden. (I

went through huge gyrations to get these 'classic wild strawberries of the European continent', only to find them highly
overrated. I was hoping for an improvement on *F. vesca*, but
moschatas have the same awful – reminds me of fake grape
flavoring – taste, dammit.)

For years I got my tree from an ill-managed planting of
Scotch pines (*Pinus sylvestris*) in a large tract right here on the
Point, carefully justifying my theft by taking trees that were
crowding others. I get a tree that requires no pruning to fit
against the wall and in turn the owner gets her stand managed, was how I always saw it. But budworm (and I think
acid rain) stopped me where conscience probably never
would have. Each year the poor trees, never seen, never
tended, are a little more sickly and yellowish. So now I am an
upright citizen and buy one from the tree farm up by the
highway. They have pines but I've switched to balsam fir,
(*Abies balsamea*), Maine's Christmas classic for its dark color,
fine fragrance and soft flat needles that cling to the branches
for a long time after the tree is cut. Absent Christmas, fir is a
trash tree around here, a fast growing opportunist of recent
clearcuts, good only for pulp. You have to prune patiently
for about a decade to get the lush conicality demanded by the
Yuletide trade. This year's selection – a seven-footer, as tall as
the little living room will take – was so thick with branches I
forewent the tinsel as there was nowhere and no way to drape
it.

I always have a decorating party to get the thing up and
trimmed, baking a humongous assortment of cookies and
inviting my closest friends Alan and Monika Magee and
Chris and Rosee Glass. Sometimes others come as well but
this year it was just us. Chris always puts up the lights,
something he once made the mistake of being very good at so
now he's stuck. Everyone jokes because I am *quite* the mar-
tinet and explain for the umpteenth time in a stern voice
exactly how things are to be done so the tree looks just so.

(Start near the trunk with the plain ornaments, wire on the antique ones very firmly, one piece of tinsel at a time, no throwing the tinsel, etc.) Chris says I missed my calling and should have been a first-grade teacher.

But first there is the gingerbread. Before the party I make lots and lots of disks of hard gingerbread, 3½ or 4 inches in diameter, hole in the top edge for hanging up. Also what I call iron icing (the decorator frosting made of eggwhite and powdered sugar) which is put in small plastic baggies. As soon as the guests show up and before things get too merry I slice a tiny corner from the bags so they act as icing cones and everybody decorates several cookies. Alan, being a painter, surprises no one by doing marvellous drawings – usually of vaguely sinister Christmas characters like evil elves. But the year Chris and Rosee went to sing in Russia (a Rachmaninoff liturgy that hadn't been performed since 1911) Chris, who's an architect, did a bunch of Eastern Orthodox churches and views of Moscow that were really a treat. (It's easy-psychology time when those two show slides of their trips. Her pictures are always of people, markets, gardens, land-scapes, his are just as invariably of walls, stairways, win-dows, occasionally whole façades or entire buildings.) The icing hardens while we eat and drink and get the basics on and by then the cookies are dry enough to hang (gingerly) with the other ornaments.

All this seems mighty far away from the garden but that's one of the great pleasures of gardening where it gets seriously cold. (A friend once sent me a book on 'cold climate garden-ing' written by a woman in ?shire. (Can't remember exactly where and the book is at the summer house.) It is to laugh. In a place like this, where it's well below freezing for weeks on end and not infrequently well below zero for several days at a stretch, there is actually about a month when you don't have to even think about the whole subject. At all. But that's it. Seed catalogues used to come in late January but now they overlap Christmas, the first of them coming right before the holiday then a deluge starting right after it. I used to resent this, same as I resent the ubiquitous Christmas decorations arriving earlier each year. Don't know how this works in England but here it just keeps getting weirder. When I was a kid the tinsel and Santas didn't go up until December. About fifteen years ago they started appearing before Thanksgiving; now they're in place side by side with the pumpkins and witches of Halloween.

Anyway, this extended Yuletide still drives me nuts but I've come to appreciate having to think about seeds right away while the eggnog is still in the glass and the wreath hanging at the door. It makes the transition back into daily life not just okay but a pleasure. There speaks the fanatic, I suppose. The thrill of seeing those little brown bits of nothing eventually emerge, after weeks and weeks, as little *green* bits of nothing is pretty sedate as thrills go. And you have to be a real gambler to appreciate the crapshoot aspect: will these tomatoes turn out to be as delicious and productive as the catalogue promises? (Probably not.) Will these exotic perennials germinate before the turn of the century? (Possibly, but don't count on it.) Will these special white variants of standard flowers actually be white? (Only about half the time, usually the half where it doesn't matter. White poppies (*Papaver somniferum*) in the vegetable beds are more or less gratifying, it's true, but a really lush, two years in the making, 5' tall, 4' wide, 20' long ribbon of white foxgloves at the edge of one's white garden that turns out to be the usual assortment of foxglove colors is – well, you may imagine I was less than pleased, the more as of course nobody viewing its admitted gorgeousness understood why I was so put out.) But there keep being things like this year's white *Venidium fastuosum* (from Thompson and Morgan) so I keep coming back for more.

They have a black and white dianthus, too, that looks

Camellia Adolphe Audusson
first flower January 17

stunning in its cover photo. I'm a total sucker for black and all approximations thereof and this latest snare and delusion would have snagged me anyway because I have some lovely black and white columbines that although needless to say are more of a dark purple – the spur petals – and cream are nevertheless among my favourite plants. Don't know their name or variety except that they're certainly not hybrids – got the seeds from Monika who doesn't remember where she got hers. The plant is refined and compact and the foliage is very dark with a definite blue cast. Want some? Lord knows it sets buckets of seed if permitted and as I keep not getting around to moving the gone-wild tall white columbines from the opposite end of the property over near these where they belong there are no other colors to cloud the issue and they should breed more or less true.

Offering the columbines, telling of my latest entrapment by the catalogues I am reminded that I am that most *declassé* of gardeners – the random collector. Something looks good, I buy it. Somebody offers me a treat, I take it. *Then* I figure out (or try to) where the hell to put it. As a result my garden is about four-fifths holding plots for experiments and only one-fifth proper garden. Makes me ache to start anew. I have fantasies alternately of bulldozers and moving – preferably to a warmer climate – but that fades once the spring's flowers start blooming and the garden that already grows starts needing attention . . . Afraid what needs attention right away is work, so will close. Promise to write again soon.

Love,

Leslie

P.S. Here's the gingerbread recipe; I bet it would be a hit at your house too. Forgive the somewhat didactic style – it's from a column.

ORNAMENTAL GINGERBREAD

This stuff is perfectly edible, containing no weird chemicals, stabilizers or shellac. But it smells a lot better than it tastes, and if you want to crunch a thick cookie you'd better have tough teeth.

For approximately 5 pounds of dough, enough for at least 60 large Christmas Ball disk cookies, a family's worth of assorted sculptures, or a few cookies each for every holiday in the year (it keeps forever in the freezer):

7 to 9 cups all-purpose flour
1 tablespoon plus 2 teaspoons ginger
1 tablespoon cinnamon
2 teaspoons *each* mace and cloves
1 teaspoon *each* baking soda, salt and cardamom
1⅔ cups solid shortening or 2 cups butter (butter smells and tastes better but doesn't keep as long)

2¼ cups unsulphured molasses
1 cup *each* white and dark brown sugar
baking parchment for the cookie sheets

Combine 5 cups of the flour with the ginger, cinnamon, mace, cloves, soda, salt and cardamom. Set aside.

Put the shortening, molasses, white and brown sugars in a large, heavy kettle (saucepan) over medium low heat. Cook, stirring, only until the fat has melted and the mixture is smooth. Don't let it simmer or the finished dough will be dry and tough.

Remove the kettle from the heat, stir in the spiced flour, and allow the mixture to cool until it is barely tepid. Slowly stir in additional flour until you have a smooth, soft, slightly greasy dough that does not stick to your hands when manipulated. Be sparing with the flour; the dough will stiffen as it cools.

Allow the dough to cool to room temperature before use, and keep wrapped tightly in plastic to avoid drying out.

Cookie sculptures should not be more than ½ inch thick, and thickness should be fairly even as little pointy parts tend to burn. Build the sculptures right on parchment, always moisten two parts to be joined, and don't forget to leave a place or two for the hanging thread. Bake thin pieces as below, thick ones at 325 for about 25 minutes.

Christmas ball (or other flat, cut-out) *cookies* Roll dough ⅛-inch thick between sheets or waxed paper. Peel off a sheet, reverse dough onto baking parchment and remove the other sheet. Use a coffee can for large round disks, whatever other cutters you like. Remove and reroll excess dough. Slide parchment on to cookie sheets and bake in a 350-degree oven for about 14 minutes or until color has changed slightly and surface looks dry.

While the cookies are still warm and soft, use a matchstick

to make a hole for the string. Remember to keep the hole at least ⅓ inch in from the edge of the cookie. Cool on racks and decorate with Iron Icing (below).

Decorative embellishments raisins, red hots, colored sugars and silver and gold dragees are the most common, but don't forget whole cloves, whole star anise, dried rosebuds and lavender flowers (available at some florists and hobby stores, if you forgot to dry your own last summer). Pictures to paste on to the icing can be cut from magazines or wrapping paper, but the easiest thing to use are paper stickers.

IRON ICING

Is made by beating an egg white until loosened, then stirring in confectioner's sugar until icing is achieved. The mixture will be lumpy at first, then smooth out. Keep it on the flowy side to coat cookies with an even sheet of white. Continue to add sugar until the lifted spoon leaves a thin trail on top of the mass if you want decorating icing that won't sag or run.

Plastic sandwich bags are ideal decorating bags, inexpensive and disposable. Use the kind with square corners and don't fill more than one-third full. Snip a *tiny* triangle from one corner, twist the top of the bag securely and squeeze out a line of icing with which to draw, write, squiggle or dot as the Christmas spirit moves you.

12 February 1990

Dear Leslie,

Food still fights its way to the forefront. Last time I wrote about the tubers of *Tropaeolum tuberosum*. Since writing I have looked it up and found that it is called Ysano in Peru, Chile and Bolivia where it is eaten like a small sweet potato. My book adds that the flavour is said to be disagreeable (they hadn't tried it). The challenge was irresistible; boiled or roasted I found it quite palatable. Perhaps my powers of self-deception are well developed for the other three people I tried it on were not impressed. Next year I shall have loads and will try serving it in various ways.

My other food event came about like this. We have invested in a leaf shredder to help us get rid of leaf-mountains that build up at the beginning of winter. The main purpose is to stop us burning off leaves and so causing yet more damage to our long-suffering environment. The results of our Kemp (American made) shredder have been excellent – a fine mulch of thumb-nail-sized bits of leaves, but (and at last I come to the point) the pile heated up in two days to what felt like a terrific temperature. So I resolved to try an experiment. Years and years ago my uncle Frank cooked a ham in a hay box and we duly ate it for Sunday lunch at a massed gathering of the cousins. What hot hay can do cannot hot leaves achieve? I went to our local butcher and bought a ten-pound piece of ham, or more properly bacon as it had already been salted and a little smoked. It was in a plastic bag. I buried it two feet down in our heap, having first made a couple of small holes in the bag to stop it exploding. My uncle had told me that it takes about two weeks to cook a ham in hay, but my patience ran out after about four days and I dug it up. *It was cooked.* In fact I think it was chronically overcooked by the way it fell off the bone.

It was very good. Daughter Phoebe (seven) was full of praise. Amy (four) was not so keen: I suspect it was much too salty for her virgin palate. I had a moment's panic after we had all eaten it, remembering all the publicity about salmonella and the way things should be cooked to a very high temperature, but all was well.

21 February Late-night musings:

I've just seen Sylvester Stallone's mother of all people on the dreaded box. She said that her son came to her when he couldn't make it with a woman and that she counselled him. I feel that for sex to work there must be a fundamental desire, and although the desire is instinctive I have always presumed that it is really a desire towards procreation, a desire that usually masquerades under the name 'love', that is the essential ingredient for sexual compatibility. I accept that there is also lust in the simple sense, otherwise how could one explain prostitution? Maybe this sounds a bit moralistic, but it's the way it strikes me.

Back to the garden. Camellias are one of the corner-stones of our garden; we have more than a hundred different cultivars. From October to April there are always plants in flower – starting with the rather tender *sasanquas* which go through until Christmas. Then in January the *japonicas* start up. They make a terrific mass of colour more and more coming into flower week by week. If there is a frost they just go dormant: the flowers that are out are burnt but the buds just wait until it warms up and then start again. The main area that I have the camellias in has a carpet of wild primroses as an underplanting. They also have been in flower for months and look like going on and on. Primroses love it in our city atmosphere, each year I split up the clumps and get about twenty-five new plants from each. Three years ago someone gave me two plants, so now I have hundreds and hundreds. I love them and as they love the garden there is total compatibility – of course linked to fecundity.

N

BED 6: THE CAMELLIA BED

SHRUBS

A = *Acer japonicum*
B = *Acer negundo* 'Elegans'
C = *Acer saccarhinum* 'Laciniatum'
D = *Arundinaria fortunei*
E = *Arundinaria murielae*
F = *Arundinaria nitida*
G = *Berberis darwinii*
H = *Buxus sempervirens* 'Elegantissima'
I = *Camellia* 'Adolphe Audusson'
J = *Camellia* 'Adolphe Audusson' (a white blotched sport)
K = *Camellia* 'Ama No Kawa'
L = *Camellia* 'Apollo'
M = *Camellia* 'Arejishi'
N = *Camellia* 'Ballet Queen'
O = *Camellia* 'Betty Sheffield'
P = *Camellia* 'Bob's Tinsie'
Q = *Camellia* 'Christmas Beauty'

R = *Camellia* 'Citation'
S = *Camellia* 'Contessa Lavinia Maggi'
T = *Camellia* 'Cornish Snow'
U = *Camellia cuspidata*
V = *Camellia* 'Dear Jenny'
W = *Camellia* 'Debutante'
X = *Camellia* 'Donation'
Y = *Camellia* 'Emmet Barnes'
Z = *Camellia* 'E. G. Waterhouse Variegata'
AA = *Camellia* 'E. G. Waterhouse'
AB = *Camellia* 'E. T. R. Carlyon'
AC = *Camellia* 'Francis Hanger'
AD = *Camellia* 'Grand Slam'
AE = *Camellia* 'Guest of Honour'
AF = *Camellia* 'Inspiration'
AG = *Camellia* 'Kramers Supreme'
AH = *Camellia* 'Lady Clare'
AI = *Camellia* 'Lasca Beauty'
AJ = *Camellia* 'Margaret Davis'
AK = *Camellia* 'Mathotiana Rosea'
AL = *Camellia* 'Matterhorn'
AM = *Camellia* 'Melody Lane'
AN = *Camellia* 'Miss Universe'
AO = *Camellia* 'Nagasaki'
AP = *Camellia saluenensis*
AQ = *Camellia sasanqua* 'Hugh Evans'
AR = *Camellia* 'Snow Goose'
AS = *Camellia* 'Tiffany'
AT = *Camellia* 'Tiptoe'
AU = *Camellia* 'Tomorrow's Dawn'
AV = *Camellia* 'Vittorio Emmanuelle II'
AW = *Camellia* 'White Fishtail'
AX = *Caryopteris* × *clandonensis*
AY = *Ceanothus dentatus*
AZ = *Ceanothus* 'Frosty Blue'
BA = *Ceanothus impressus*
BB = *Ceanothus* 'Italian Skies'
BC = *Ceanothus verrucosus*
BD = *Chaenomeles speciosa*
BE = *Euonymus japonicus*
BF = *Euonymus* 'President Gauthier'
BG = *Forsythia* 'Lynwood'
BH = *Hamamelis* × *intermedia* 'Jelena'
BI = *Hydrangea* 'Kluis Superba'

BJ = *Hydrangea* 'Lilacina'
BK = *Mahonia* 'Charity'
BL = *Populus alba* 'Richardii'
BM = *Pyracantha* 'Watereri'
BN = Rose 'Chinatown'
Rose 'General Schablikine'
Rose 'Mme Edouard Herriot'
Rose 'Morning Jewel'
BO = Rose Nevada
BP = *Senecio greyi* (*Brachyglottis greyi*)
BQ = *Senecio rotundifolia* (*Brachyglottis rotundifolia*)
BR = *Spirea thunbergii*
BS = *Viburnum tinus*

PERENNIALS

I have not drawn the plants in but just marked the spots

CA = *Agapanthus umbellatus*
CB = *Campanula lactiflora*
CD = *Chelidonium majus*, the wild Greater Celandine
CE = *Crocosmia* × *crocosmiiflora*, the common montbretia
CF = *Hemerocallis fulva*, the common Day Lily
CG = *Echium pininana*
CH = *Hosta sieboldiana*
CI = *Impatiens glandulifera*, the Policeman's Helmet
CJ = *Lamium galeobdolon* 'Variegatum'
CK = *Macleaya cordata*, the Plumed Poppy
CL = *Tropaeolum* 'Jewel Mixed', the common nasturtium
CM = *Tropaeolum tuberosum* 'Ken Aslet'
CN = *Phygelius aequalis*
CO = *Primula vulgaris*, the common primrose
CP = *Pulmonaria*

I've got a yellow area in the garden, but as yet it is not a great success. It is mainly foliage – golden philadelphus, spirea, hops, berberis and maple, then patches of flower – roses, gladioli, broom, etc. This year I am trying to improve it and make it really work. I have gone mad on lilies almost all yellow but with a few whites as well to break up and thus show off the yellows: 'Connecticut King' and Citronella strain for the yellow, with *Lilium* 'Mont Blanc' and *Galtona candicans*, the summer hyacinth, for the whites. I am also planning on some perennials, when the plants become available: a patch of *Coreopsis verticillata* which I hope will stay in flower for months, also *Campanula* 'Dickson's Gold', and then poking through them some *Crocosmia* 'Solfatare'. I am not convinced that even this lot will be an unbridled success. Do you have any favourite yellow perennials that come leaping to mind? All help gratefully received.

By the way do you remember months ago you wrote about *Acidanthera*? Well we now have some in the garden but it wasn't me who planted them. Beryl Pye (she really is a sweetie pie) planted them: she has a corner of the garden that she completely looks after herself – a sort of cottage garden within the garden.

Sorry to be so long replying but I am invaded. *Herbs*, the next book, has just been pasted-up – the colour proofs went back to the publisher yesterday – and now we are already deep into doing the paste-up of the *Mushrooms of North America* for Little Brown. A thousand pictures!

Love,

Roger

Cushing, Maine

February 15 1990

11 pm

Dear Roger,

I've spent the last hour or so starting the first seeds, am dead tired but thought of you keenly as this is the official start of my garden year. It's too early to do the bulk of it, but leeks, onions, pansies and a few other items (such as cardoons and *Salvia patens*) must be begun now if they are to perform well when the time comes.

Leslie

It's completely quiet, hasn't been a car by since dinner time, the phone silent. Peace. Outside the back door the snow is pale grey and smooth. Just stopped coming down a little while ago after falling for two days, most of the time right at the edge between snow and freezing rain. It has built an almost lacquered surface, glazed and shining rather than fluffy and sparkly. Shadows are deep, blue and charcoal and near-on black. From the chicken house to the back door, one pure diagonal line of dots – courtesy someone's little cat feet – each dot brilliant, an almost painful silvery white in the lamplight from the windows.

Sweet dreams,

Leslie

Cushing, Maine

Dear Roger,

Right drove up just now so can't truly answer your wonderful letter/packet of goodies but did want you to know they'd arrived. (I'll pass on the *Sutherlandia montana* seeds to somebody in a warmer climate. 'Hardy to −5°' means 'won't winter over' around here.)

Don't know if the enclosed catalogue of hot and ornamental peppers by 'The Pepper Gal' will be of interest as you can see she's rather haphazard – but it does give an idea of what's available. Is all your research for the vegetable book already done? (that's my specialty, you know).

Or maybe you don't know. My flowers get photographed a lot, and most of the garden writing I do is about ornamentals these days. But I started gardening for purely utilitarian purposes – in order to get the best, most interesting vegetables, fruits and herbs. Food gardening was my introduction to the art and my *first* Maine garden hardly had any flowers in it at all.

I did do a lot of carpet bedding with the vegetables; perhaps by way of compensation. There were zigzag borders of leeks, with the triangular patches filled by assorted lettuces. Beds of fennel were ringed with rhubarb chard, and I got a lot of mileage out of seaweed mulch – the black is very effective.

There's a fellow on our road who is a perfect carpet gardener of the old school. His whole front yard is filled with patterns and (except for the sunflowers) flat as the proverbial pancake. Plastic doodads are minimal, he does it all with flowers: zinnias, snapdragons, impatiens, petunias, dusty miller – the year before last he spelled out HELLO! in yellow and orange marigolds (yellow on an orange ground). Rather like an Escher in that you didn't really see it until it was pointed out to you then you couldn't *not* see it. This year yielded no similar splendor but I have hopes for next. Doesn't do to be snobby, though – I think we all start out as naive painters and only move to Impressionism after a bit of practice.

Truth be told, I sort of miss carpet bedding, but not as much as I miss my mother's Pennsylvanian gardens, where I played as a child and which I can see from the few pictures that exist were very gracefully designed. All I can remember directly are the hollyhocks against the silvery rail fence, the stream that flowed down one side of the vegetable garden in a rock-lined channel, and Japanese beetles which I 'helped' by picking in hundreds from the roses. The roses I don't remember at all, but those beetles are as clear as yesterday.

And so is the quality of the food – simple salads of sliced tomatoes, sweet, tender corn on the cob, lettuces of astonishing crispness and depth of flavor. I missed vegetables like that my whole adult life, but I made do with what the markets offered until I came to Maine, where pure necessity forced me back to the garden at last.

When I moved here in 1972 the only way to get eggplant was to grow it. Ditto fresh herbs. Twenty years ago the way to cook with fresh basil, dill or coriander was to grow your own; the only way to get a summer squash smaller than a baseball bat was to pick one from your own plants. Farmstands were few, far-between and ill-stocked.

They still are, when you think about the riches available through seed catalogues. For the first few years, I just went to the local nurseries and bought seedlings. Then I caught on to starting from seeds, began running tomato trials, comparing the different breeds of bell peppers, ordering exotic potatoes. So if you need some pictures of or information about weird edibles, maybe I can help.

Off tomorrow a.m. for Philadelphia to be a visiting

luminary at 'the Book and Cook', a big restaurant promotion they (the city) put on every year.

As soon as I get home, copy editing of *The Modern Country Cook* for work, and for fun writing to Roger. Hope all's well with you and yours.

X X Leslie

P.S. 'drove up' is Maine slang for totally busy.

Cushing, Maine

Well my dear I scarcely know where to start so I will start at starting, since that's pretty much what's going on around here. There's still a bit of snow in the shady places and heavy, wet snow is predicted for tomorrow, but the catkins are silvery velveting out on the pussy-willows, the first crocus are blooming and assorted early narcissi have buds. Tulips are still pretty low to the ground. Greening-up has just begun. The lawns are still more brown than otherwise and there is mud everywhere.

Spring as usual: it's cold and raw and highly suggestive of going to Florida except that you have to be here so you can get going with the seedlings. Our season is so short even tough things like asters and snapdragons are best begun at least eight weeks before planting out. March and April mean a fridge top paved with pots, crowded babies awaiting transplant lining every windowsill. I rent space to grow stuff on at a greenhouse in Camden (about half an hour up the road) but the house is still littered with seedling impedimenta because I do most of the actual work in the kitchen – employing the shining hours of early morning when I'm still too fuddled to write.

A greater concentration on perennials and shrubbery would certainly alleviate the burden; our climate limits the options less than you might think. Mahonia, for instance, usually sold as berberis here, is quite hardy in most of its varieties even in Maine. But I got started this way as a result of being a renter and have remained a real sucker for annual flowers. And since I'm also more or less the vegetable queen there's not really much help for it.

This year I'm trying a new datura, *D. suaveolens*, which is supposed to be extremely tall and very fragrant. Alas, germination looks doubtful. Also a new salpiglossis called 'Kew Blue', to be known as 'Salpiglossis Last Chance'. For several years now every kind of salpiglossis I've tried has failed to produce the gorgeous dark browns and violets that are the whole point of the plant. Instead, I mostly get dingy mustard yellow flowers in which the characteristic gold veins are lost. If the 'Kew Blues' don't perform I'm going to admit salpiglossi are nothing but uppity petunias and say the hell with it. Will spare you further annuals list; there are *dozens* even though each year I swear I'm going to go in for something recherché and difficult in a different way (like species clematis) instead.

I'm also trying to cut down on vegetable varieties, but new enticements make that hard. This year's flings will include – just started the seeds today – 'Evergreen' tomatoes, still green when ripe. They should go well with the proven 'Lemon Boy' (yellow), 'Zapotec Pink' (an heirloom that's actually a rather creepy green-flashed pale magenta) and White Beauty (which really is). The 'Beauty' is also one delicious tomato you bet, and a very long keeper. By the time they're fully ripe they've turned a lovely shade of creamy ivory and they encourage me in the matter of the 'Evergreens', proving as they do that odd color doesn't preclude fine flavor. Speaking of which, allow me (in case I haven't already done so) to recommend 'Brandywine', unquestionably the tastiest tomato I grow. Of course, that's the extent of its virtues – it's late, shy bearing, prone to cat-facing . . .

April 12

But maybe I shouldn't go on about tomatoes (perhaps one thing that does better here than there?), since among the seedlings in the garden there are a lot more flowers than food. Many are perennials I either can't afford or have trouble finding in nursery catalogues, things like the yellow delphinium, *D. zalil*, and tree dahlias (from J. L. Hudson Co., no Latin name supplied, seed claimed to have been collected from the wild in Mexico). Tree dahlias are supposed to eventually reach six or seven feet and have dangling clusters of pink and purple bell-shaped (!) flowers. I will believe it when I see it which to date I have not done. (Catalogue not illustrated.) They make gorgeous foliage plants, so far about five feet tall, with huge, tropical-looking but fundamentally dahlia-shaped leaves and serious trunks, complete with the appearance of bark. But they don't set much in the way of tubers, just one or two paltry lumps per plant, so although I started two years ago – this will be year three – I don't seem to be getting ahead on them. It's maddening since conventional dahlias do, if anything, too well, increasing madly like your nasturtiums. (I'm jealous of those *Tropaeolum tuberosum*, can't find a source, do please send seed if your plants set any.) There are always millions of giant dahlia tubers at the end of the season, reputedly (ahem) edible by someone besides the mice. I confess I haven't tried it yet. They're so damned prolific I can't help feeling that if they were tasty we'd know it by now. Wheelbarrows full of them, 'Free, Help Yourself', are a fairly common front-yard decoration around town in the early fall. I was going to say something about how thrifty Yankees would never give that much food away if it were any good, but wheelbarrows full of free cucumbers are also a regular feature (and almost nobody collects mushrooms).

I have given some thought to your yellow corner, an idea that struck a familiar chord. Two years ago I started building a pink and yellow 'border', actually the front section of the right hand side of the lower garden. This was inspired by the acquisition of a large, vaguely Chinese-flavoured Minton bowl, enamel yellow outside and the color of raspberry sherbet within and not even a little hideous as by rights such a combination should be extremely.

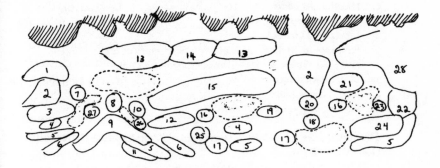

The yellow and Pink (Minton) bed, redrawn by Beow from Justin's sketch

MINTON BOWL BORDER, LOWER GARDEN

1. *Althea* (peach colored) from Beth
2. *Thermopsis caroliniana*
3. *Hemerocallis* 'Hyperion'
4. *Dianthus knappii*
5. *Dianthus plumarius* 'Old Laced Pinks'
6. *Heuchera sanguinia* 'Bressingham Hybrids', selected for paler shades
7. *Phlox* 'Rosalinde'
8. *Papaver orientalis* 'Princess Victoria Louise'
9. *Korean Chrysanthemum* (pink) from Olive
10. Lily 'Parisienne'
11. *Allium roseum*
12. *Hemerocallis* 'Raja'
13. *Helianthus* from Paul
14. *Astilbe* from Paul
15. Bearded Iris (yellow) from Lois
16. *Heliopsis* 'Golden Glow'
17. *Alchemilla mollis*
18. Rose 'Amber Queen'
19. *Echinacea* 'Bravado'
20. *Phlox paniculata* (pink) from Paul

21. *Dicentra spectabilis*
22. *Monarda* (deep pink) from Bruce
23. *Ligularia* 'The Rocket'
24. *Hemerocallis* 'Stella d'Oro' and two peach-apricot mid-session
    bloomers whose names are lost in the mists of time
25. Lily 'Pink Perfection'
26. Lily 'Yellow Blaze'
27. *Filipendula* (pink) from Lois

The dotted lines are Tulips: 'Yellow Parrot', 'Apricot Beauty', 'New Design' and 'Baroness'.

In between, self-sown: *Digitalis ferruginea*, *Linaria purpurea* 'Canon J Went', *Digitalis purpurea* and *Malva sylvestris* 'Mauritiana'.

Still to come: a pink landscape rose, a test specimen from Jackson and Perkins that as yet has no name, more Echinacea plus an experimental Forsythia from plant breeder friends of Paul's.

So, in addition to the plants you mention, what about our dooryard staple forsythia and what about witch hazel? And *Clematis tangutica* (love them yellow bells). Things like Welsh poppies (*Meconopsis cambrica*) and Lady's Mantle (*Alchemilla mollis*) probably are such a given that they're not worth mentioning but they sure put out a lot of yellow down there in the lower regions. You didn't mention iris but the yellow ones here (nameless gift from a friend of Lois's) look very good with the bleeding heart and pinks, and the foliage stays a nice bit of pale orderliness as the summer blowse progresses. Ligularia? My garden is too dry and sunny for this wide-leaved wonder to flourish but I seem to remember you saying you had some. I can't grow Japanese iris, either, to my everlasting regret. *Dianthus knapii*, on the other hand, is very happy here. Bloom season isn't as long as the pink pinks' but they will rebloom in fall if cut back hard.

Do you know *Thermopsis carolina*? It's a pea-relative with lupin-like, pale yellow flowers. Blooming period is pretty short but the foliage is dainty, pretty and long-lasting, a nice bright sort of poison green. And I'm a big fan of *Digitalis lutea*, happily perennial here and a mad self-seeder (but easy to weed out). The foliage is very unlike regular foxglove foliage, almost strap-shaped, dark green and shiny. The flowers are quite small, somewhere between gold and brass with a dusting of brown spots. Height seems quite variable, so far I've had 'em anywhere from three to five feet. One of the best things about them is the bee-bump. Bumblebees love them but can't quite get inside, so all summer there is reliably a chance to view the flowers looking like sacks-of-something-that-wiggles, with bee-butts barely protruding from the open ends.

Speaking of splendors given to self-sowing, I can't find that winter heliotrope in any of my catalogues. It certainly sounds delightful and might well be less rambunctious in our harsher climate (probably, knowing my luck, it'll be one more thing to 'treat as annual' and start in a little pot every spring).

And thinking of self-seeding brings me to your story about Mr Stallone (great name, under the circumstances). Rather a wow that he brings his impotence problems to his mother – and perhaps indicative of why he's got 'em. Can't read a crucial word here. Did she 'counsel' him, 'console' him, or something else entirely?

A complex problem, and as you mention, quite a difference between long-term compatability ('love') and the simple desire loosely defined as 'lust'. Speaking for myself, I can't say the latter feels indissolubly tied to the former. It's hard to know for sure – in my case both suitable partners for the one and likely targets? objects? recipients? of the other have been scarce unto nonexistent for years – but as far as I can tell, desire is just linked to general mood (I'm horny when I'm happy) and that, in turn, is linked to all the usual cues (accomplishment, affection etc.) and also very importantly to light. There's an enormous need, especially about this time of year when there has been long deprivation, to feel

Chrysanthemum X superbum 'Elisabeth'

Lysimachia clethroides

Rodgersia sambucifolia

the sun on my naked body. Usually, thank goodness, at some point in April there's finally at least one day when it's warm enough to take off all my clothes and go lie on the back porch, legs open, getting everything bathed in/by those rays ... Not something I'd want to try in lower latitudes but sunburn is seldom a problem in Maine even in high summer.

Just looked up from the page: it's snowing, so I guess it's still sublimation-in-food time. I'm trying to eat up the last of the summer garden stuff from the freezer. Yellow squash with sugarsnap peas and basil, stewed tomatoes with grilled peppers and coriander and baby purple onions, harvest stew full of snap and shell beans, zucchini, peppers, squash blossoms and cream. A funny diet as the first asparagus comes into the stores, but the first asparagus won't come into the garden for at least a month and when it does I want to face the new season with a clean slate (and a clean freezer).

More soon, the Easter baking is calling. Feel like it would be nice to send fancy egg breads to the folks of Eastern Europe, especially Russia, where they've still got such a long,

weary way to comfortable abundance (and such a long tradition of festive baking for this holiday). Come to think of it, I
wish I could send a nice plump, fruit-studded Kulich to *you*,
and hope all is well in (good grief, a head tax!) your part of
the world.
Love,

Leslie

26 April 1990

Leslie,

A great letter, lots of things I must respond to, but first the realization has finally hit me that you are the queen of vegetables and a princess of annuals!

Three volumes are already out in the series of books on garden plants I am doing with Martyn Rix – *Bulbs*, *Roses* and *Shrubs*. *Perennials* we are just finishing off for delivery in May. This will be followed by *Vegetables*, *Conservatory Plants* and then *Annuals*, hopefully one a year over the next three years. We are and have been working on all three for the past couple of years so now it is down to (in the case of vegetables anyway) finding the exciting rarities. You sound as if you have lots! Exciting! We need photographs!

I'm going to be boring and tell you how I do my shots to ensure success.

HERE BEGINNETH THE FIRST LESSON:

Do a bracket on all exposures. Do what the meter tells you to do, i.e. f11 at 1/60th of a second, then do a half stop lighter, then a stop lighter, i.e. f8/11 at 1/60th and f8 at 1/60th, then half stop and whole stop darker i.e. f11/16 and f16 at 1/60th. This may sound a bit tricky but in fact once you're set up you can just crack through by using the aperture ring. In fact I do it by feel and so the shots only take about as long as it takes to wind on.

When choosing transparencies (it must be slide film) it is often the case that a darker exposure is better for reproduction. This is especially true in the case of white flowers; the only sort of tranny good enough to reproduce from has to have detail in the whites. This will almost certainly mean that the foliage will be on the dark side. When taking dark objects like black flowers the opposite will be true. The meter in your camera is a mindless moron and must be kept under control: all professionals do brackets as they *know* they can't take a perfect exposure, only amateurs can do that with one frame. Although it sounds expensive (film costs go up by ×5) it means you will get usable results every time.

LESSON THE SECOND:

Use a slow colour film like Kodak Ektachrome 100ASA or Kodachrome. The slower the film the more body there is in the colour, known as colour density or saturation. This slower film will mean that the exposures will be more difficult so in some instances you will need a tripod. A still like a bunch of potatoes can then be shot with a longer exposure time, say 1/8 or 1/4 second. This sort of exposure time will of course be no good for flowers growing as you will get wind movement, but when doing flowers growing you will need all the depth of field you can get (this is achieved by stopping down, i.e. f16 in preference to say f8). So you will

Fill the frame as this

still be helped by a tripod so that you can shoot at say 1/30th second or even (in low wind conditions) 1/15th.

Please will you shoot some of your wild-sounding vegetables for us? They should be done on a background of clean earth or stone or something very simple and kitchen garden-ish. If there is a detail that does not show, say pink-fleshed potatoes, could you just shoot say half a dozen but cut one in half to show the flesh? They should not be small in the frame but nearly fill it so that there is greater detail to reproduce from.

LESSON THE THIRD: LIGHT

Harsh sunlight is too contrasty, especially for still life, best shot on a day with thin cloud cover. If the sun always shines in Maine a help would be to use a white card as a 'fill-in'; this is to reflect some light back into the shadow areas so that you don't end up with a shot that has bleached highlights and black shadows with no detail – even Rembrandt with his extremes of *chiaroscuro* had detail in the shadows. With flowers growing, however, this need not apply. If they look great in the natural light they will look great when shot.

Again though, if you shoot against the light, i.e. with sunlight coming through the flowers, make sure to do the darkest of the bracket as the sunlight will tend to flare the film and make the result lighter than the meter tells you. (I am presuming that you have a camera that you can operate manually.)

Now the difficult bit, how to pay you. The sums we get paid are pretty measly, somewhere in the region of $20 a shot (I'm not complaining of the deal), so I won't insult you by offering that; but can I pay for film and buy you a tripod if you need one? I stress paying for the film as doing loads of shots is really the way to get good ones; each time you look over what you have done you think of new ways of getting better pictures. Also if you tackle the same subject again it pushes you into finding a new angle/viewpoint or trying a different time of day or a change of light. Basically doing lots of shots gets you in practice. Taking photographs is just like playing the piano: the more you practise, the better you shoot. (When I say I will pay for film I don't mean only film that might be of use to me in a book, I mean all the film you need.)

My yellow flower bed backs on to the tennis court so it has twelve-foot-high netting at the back up which run roses, clematis, golden hops, etc. It is a very sunny spot overlooking the main lawn where people sit in summer. (We are having summer now, the temperature goes up to around 75°F every day and only down to about 52°F at night.) Anyway, my system is that in the beds that you see from the lawns in summer I try to plant things for summer effect, and the beds seen from the outside and the main path I plant more with spring things. The above is my explanation of why no forsythia or witch hazel, but *Clematis tangutica* is a lovely thought. Also, I haven't put in Welsh poppies (I have some seed). Ligularia is also a good idea although, like your garden, it may be too dry; but I shall add them to my list. I have just done a plan of the bed so that I have a record of what is there. As you will see I have gone very strongly for yellow foliage plants and to break up the yellows I have put in quite a few white flowered things. The annuals tend to be self-seeded or otherwise scattered about so that they come up naturally through the shrubs and perennials. Inevitably I have blue larkspurs and other mismatches arriving by accident that don't fit into the scheme, but so it goes.

BED 25: THE YELLOW BED

1. Rose 'Maigold'
2. Rose 'Handel'
3. Rose 'Mme Isaac Pereire'
4. *Humulus lupulus* 'Aureus'
5. Rose 'Casino'

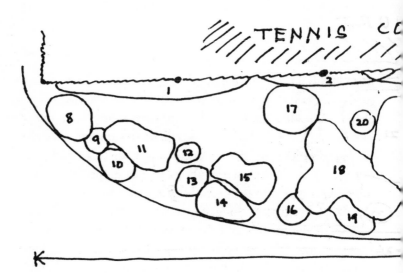

6. *Clematis alpina*
7. Rose 'Autumn Sunlight'
8. *Spirea thunbergii*
9. *Ribes sanguineum* 'Brocklebankii'
10. *Phlomis fruticosa*
11. *Euonymus fortunei* 'Emerald 'n' Gold'
12. Rose 'Graham Thomas'
13. *Melissa officinalis* 'Variega'
14. *Phlomis fruticosa*
15. *Berberis thunbergii* 'Aurea'
16. *Abutilon* 'Canary Bird'
17. *Acer japonica* 'Aurea'
18. *Berberis thunbergii* 'Aurea'
19. *Melissa* 'Variegata'
20. Rose 'Yellow Charles Austin'
21. *Physocarpus opulifolius* 'Darts Gold'
22. *Melissa officinalis* 'Aurea'
23. *Artemisia lactiflora*
24. Tuberous begonias (yellow)
25. Rose 'Yellow Charles Austin'
26. Rose 'Lady Hillingdon' Climber
27. *Lilium* 'Connecticut King'

28. *Anthemis tinctoria*
29. *Lilium* 'Sunray'
30. *Calendula*
31. *Alstroemeria* 'Ligtu Hybrids'
32. *Lilium* 'Citronella Strain'
33. *Filipendula ulmaria* 'Aurea'
34. *Lilium* 'Mont Blanc'
35. Tulip 'West Point'
36. *Calendula*
37. *Weigela Looymansii* 'Aurea'
38. *Helichrysum* 'Sulphur light'
39. *Coreopsis verticillata*
40. *Lilium* 'Citronella Strain'
41. *Lilium* 'Connecticut King'
42. *Lilium* 'Connecticut King'
43. *Melissa* 'Aurea'
44. Rose 'Lawrence Johnston' Climber
45. *Gaillardia* 'Aurea'
46. *Filipendula ulmaria* 'Aurea'
47. *Spirea* 'Gold Flame'
48. *Galtonia candicans*
49. *Lilium* 'Connecticut King'
50. Rose 'English Garden'
51. *Origanum onites* 'Aureum'
52. *Sagina glabra* 'Aurea'
53. *Lilium* 'Connecticut King'
54. *Philadelphus coronarius* 'Aureus'
55. *Catalpa bignonoides* 'Aurea'
56. Tulip 'West Point'
57. *Calendula*
58. *Cytisus* × *kewensis*

There is a yellow leaved Fuchsia which I want for the gap above 12/15

ANNUALS IN BETWEEN:

Cosmos 'Sunny Gold'
Cosmos 'Candy Stripe'
Eschscholzia 'Sundew'
Oenothera
Chrysanthemum parthenium 'Aureum'
Consolida ambigua
Physalis alkekengi

On 2 May I will be giving a lecture at the London Museum. They are having a History of London Gardens exhibition all summer and I'm to do a talk on Eccleston Square. (Pay £60, cost of me making slides about £120.) I must be mad but I am quite looking forward to it and it gives me another chance to moan on about the ruddy car park developers. Also I am driven to crystallize my thoughts and philosophy on gardening (too big a word for having ideas).

Loved your thoughts on love in the light/lust in the dust. Hot sun, I agree, is the great aphrodisiac, but then close runners are good food, and of course drink. But after all that there has to be something special there doesn't there?

Love,

Roger

Cushing, Maine

Dear Roger,

Thanks for your letter. The diagram of the yellow border is fascinating and the photographic encouragements just that. I'm still camera-shopping (like computer-shopping it's quite the undertaking and could easily eat up a person's life if she weren't so pressed to do six thousand other things, most of them equally expensive and even less gratifying).

I am, it's true, the queen of the annuals and vegetables, a title of dubious desirability given that there is this longish period in the beginning of the summer when a) the work-pressure is beyond belief, tray after tray of babies to plant *Right now! Yesterday! Hurry Up!* and b) the garden looks – not exactly like hell, but not exactly like a garden anyone in their right mind would be proud of. There is gorgeousness in the perennial beds – right now the columbines, pinks, coral bells and iris are blooming, foxgloves are just about to do it, delphiniums hard on their heels – but most of the garden is brown earth and weeds, with hundreds of little plants set doinkety-doinkety-doink . . . not in rows, it's not *that* dreadful, but not in close enough proximity to look anything but paltry in the extreme and as many now have their first flowers it's somehow even worse: a three-foot area with two screaming orange calendulas in it, a scattering of zinnias, here and there a white venidium (they really are going to be gorgeous, by the way, one of those rare instances where the catalogue didn't lie) and just the beginnings of lushness from the alyssum, which at this point is not a 'carpet of snow' but a scattering of loose threads.

Oh well.

Do you have raccoons in London? They do splendidly in

suburbs here and are sometimes seen in cities . . .
Come to think of it, I don't even know if
you've got the damned things in
England whatsoever. If not, be joyful.
They're most notorious for rooting
around in garbage and for eating all
the sweetcorn two days before the
ears are ripe, but they also dig up
any newly-set plant that sits
on the faintest raccoon-
nosable hint of bone
meal.

So one way and another, not much gratification just yet, especially in the edibles department. Asparagus and rhubarb (this year's recipe discovery is rhubarb and dried cherries – terrific!) are over and now it's pure leafy green – lettuces, cress, rocket, and of course lamb's quarters, an exquisitely tasty weed *much* easier to grow than spinach since not growing it would be the trick. Other People's Strawberries are starting to come in, my newly-planted 'Tristars' are looking very promising but also like at least another two weeks off.

As you describe your choices in the yellow border I realize how public your garden is, how important it is to please your fellow square-dwellers, the multitudes of passers-by, the Guardians of Ancient Trees, just about everybody except the Queen (and for all I know, her, too). Leads me to think on the meaning of the garden as an enclosure. That's where the word comes from, after all, and for me that sense of a protected place is vital. In my case the boundaries are more psychological than physical – there are no fences or sidewalks or hedges, both of the main gardens more or less bleed off into the woods and fields – but there is a clear sense of something-within-borders because all the plantings are oriented towards the central paths. The gardens have obviously been built to be viewed from within, and this inward turning is as effective in its way as walls. You can tell right away when you first see the property that the gardens are not for public display.

And as soon as you're in either garden you can tell one vision – if it can be called that – is in charge. Some areas are very utilitarian, others quite formally designed, and not a few of the transitions are on the rough side. It's really a sort of private dialogue between myself and the plants, with classical design aesthetics relegated to the back seat.

I *do* care what Lois thinks (after all, she owns the place). It's nice to have friends in and around. And I'm vain enough to be pleased when painters want to immortalize the joint even though easels set up in the narrow paths present problems of their own.

Considering how haphazard the place is, it's gotten quite a lot of painterly attention. Lois has mostly been resistant – gardens are not her sort of landscape – but Nancy Wissemann-Widrig has become a regular visitor, her husband, John Wisseman, paints here from time to time, and so do others from the area.

After a while, they add up. A few years ago a gallery called Maine Coast Artists had a show of garden paintings and so many (6 or 7 out of about 60) were done here they had me come and give a talk about 'Art in the Garden'. Big mistake on my part. Everybody who came to the talk wanted to come see the garden. I told 'em it was better in the paintings and they shouldn't mess with their illusions.

Nancy is such a fixture at this point that, like Lois, she's

When it rains,
Nancy takes refuge
in the greenhouse

part of the garden and welcome whenever. But other than that, well, 'secret' isn't at all the right word, but I tend to be very close with the place, have never (and don't intend) to be part of the garden-club tour circuit and was *livid* the other day when a woman I'd never seen before came strolling right into the garden, about a hundred feet (through a field) from the nearest public right of way. She announced, in tones implying she expected me to be grateful, that she'd admired it (walked through it, from the sound of her) many times previously, asked a whole bunch of questions in spite of my extremely frosty responses, and then blithely announced she'd be back when it was further along, since not much seemed to happening just yet! I was too nonplussed to suggest she wait until she was invited into the equivalent of a stranger's living room. Fervently hope my coolness will be enough to discourage further intrusions. We shall see.

I still boil in retrospect, realize my attitude probably sounds churlish, if not absurd, especially to an urbanite. But as you will see when you visit, this is a very quiet, little-travelled place. During the busiest part of the day a car goes by, maybe once every twenty minutes or so in the winter, once every two or three minutes in the summer. And in both cases said car is almost always being driven by someone who lives or works or is well known on this two-mile stretch of dead-end road where there are not more than thirty-five houses *if* you count numerous summer places. People pretty much keep to themselves by unspoken but widely-understood agreement and while they feel free to do things like come to the door and ask for donations for the Cancer Society, they don't just drop in on strangers. Thank God. The woman, who has a summer house on the main road, is undoubtedly 'from away', a phrase that of course also applies to me, and to anyone else not born here. In fact, there is a famous Maine joke about the subject that I've always liked: Seems an outsider had occasion to be at the funeral of an elderly resident, a man much loved in the small fishing community where he'd lived ever since his birth. The outsider remarked to a native:

'Guess you'll really miss old Joe, he was the very best type of Mainer, wasn't he?'

'We'hnt a Mainah,' replied the native, 'his folks were from New Jehseh.'

'But I thought he was born here,' the outsider protested.

'So 'e waas,' replied the native, 'but that don't make 'im a Mainah. Yer cat can have kittens in the oven, but that don't make 'em biscuits.'

This is perhaps a bit extreme, but the basic idea is okay with me, one of the local customs that seems a bit limiting but makes its own kind of sense.

As does – to return to the garden – the local habit of planting practically the whole damn yard to lilacs and to hell with the other forty-nine weeks of the year. There's a certain sameness once the season is over, but that's actually quite restful, and during lilac time it's an overpowering intoxication. On some stretches of road – the ones lined with old farms – there are such masses of pale purple bloom the fragrance pours through the car windows even at sixty miles an hour. Nice to reflect that New England lilacs were already emblematic when Lincoln died, that they're one of those imports that has flourished here as nowhere else. I've read that the collection at Harvard's Arnold Arboretum is the largest in the world, and everyone I know describes it as a proper wonder, but lilac time is planting time and somehow I have yet to get up there and see it.

What we have here are generally the common purple kind. *Syringa vulgaris*. Most well-maintained older properties have hedges of them along at least one border and some right-thinking homeowners who don't have them to start with go ahead and plant them. Lois set a row between the house and the road when she moved here thirty years ago, along with a short hedge at her Western boundary, but I have been remiss. Currently have only one, a 'Miss Ellen Willmott' in the white garden. I've long had in mind a nice Maine-style hedgerow running down the hill between the upper garden and the lower, and just today my friend Sam, his chainsaw still running from the whacking-down of a couple of extra birch trees, pointed out that lilacs would be just right in a spot currently occupied, *faute de mieux*, by a couple of undistinguished chokecherries.

Sam has been setting his own lilac hedge, using sprouts from the property originally settled (and lilacked) by his great-great-grandfather. In Sam's case, the distance between lilacs is only a few thousand feet, but lilacs grow all over this country, a wave settled westward with the pioneers, for just Sam's good reasons. Not only are they long lived, handsome, easy to transplant and care for, they're symbolically loaded: a sprout of lilac is a coal from the home fire – guess I'll get mine from Lo's place.

I've gotten a lot of my plants from friends, a realization brought home with special force when I made the diagram of the yellow/pink bed. Compared to your elegant yellow border, it's filled with the nameless – or, more accurately, the name-unknown-to-me. It's frustrating, but names aren't everything, and when I think of things like how a rose's color may change depending on the light, the importance of pH to hydrangeas, the effect of soil fertility on plant size and vigor, documentation of the garden takes its place with musical notation, recipe-writing and choreographer's diagrams. The representation conveys such a small part of the real thing. I can't, for instance, send the baby phoebes having discussions in their nest under the eaves (they sound like they need oiling), can't send you the fragrance of night blooming stock as evening comes on, can't send the velvet feel of mullein planted too close to the path as it brushes against my bare calf. Can't send you the mosquitoes, either. Count your blessings.

PAN-FRIED SHAD (OR HERRING)
WITH RHUBARB COMPOTE

(From a column once more. Compote is also tasty with pork chops or other fatty meat – or plain, eaten with a spoon, though it's a bit intense in that mode)

For 4 servings:

¾ lb young rhubarb, trimmed but unpeeled, cut into ⅓ inch
dice, about 2 cups prepared
¼ cup (2 oz) sugar, or slightly more
⅛ teaspoon salt
1 large garlic clove, split into 4
a one-inch piece of cinnamon stick
2 slices fresh ginger, each about 1 inch in diameter and ⅛ inch
thick
¼ cup dried cherries, about 1 oz, available in natural food and
gourmet stores
1 small, barely ripe cooking pear, such as bosc, peeled, cored,
and diced slightly smaller than the rhubarb
8 slices bacon (smoked streaky)
4 medium-sized shad fillets, about 1½ lb, or the same weight
of herring fillets
cornstarch (cornflour) for dusting

Begin with the compote. Combine the rhubarb in a non-reactive bowl with the sugar and salt. Stir well, cover the bowl and let sit, stirring from time to time, for about 1½ hours or until the rhubarb has given off roughly ½ cup (¼ pint) of juice.

Put the garlic, cinnamon, ginger and cherries in a heavy

non-reactive saucepan big enough to hold the rhubarb in no more than three layers. Strain in the juice, reserving the fruit. Simmer over low heat, stirring occasionally, for about ten minutes or until the cherries are plump and the liquid is reduced to a couple of tablespoons of very thick syrup. Remove and discard garlic, ginger and cinnamon.

When the syrup is ready, add the rhubarb and pear, stir well and raise heat to low-medium. Cook, stirring often, for about eight minutes or until the rhubarb is barely softened and there is little or no free liquid in the pan. Remove from the heat, let cool a moment, then taste to see if extra sugar is needed. Puckery-sour is too sour, but don't forget this is a relish, not dessert. It will keep in the refrigerator for about two days.

To complete the dish, fry the bacon until it is crisp and drain it well, reserving the fat. Right before serving, pour enough of the clear, residue-free bacon fat into a wide frying pan to make a very generous layer, about ¼ inch. Heat until it is very hot – almost but not quite smoking.

Pat the fillets dry with paper towelling, then rub lightly with cornstarch. Slide the fish into the pan skin side down and cook, turning once, for about three minutes a side. Fillets should be lightly brown and slightly crisp on the outside, just done within. If the fat is both deep and hot they will not be greasy, but they should be briefly drained on absorbent paper to wick off any external oiliness.

Serve at once on warmed plates, garnished with the reserved bacon and accompanied by the compote. Parsleyed new potatoes go well with this.

So would a parsnip and potato purée.

Historical note (possibly apocryphal): some sources mention a Micmac Indian legend concerning the origin of the shad, an extraordinarily bony fish. Seems there was a porcupine discontented with his lot who asked the Great Spirit Manitou for a better situation. Ever obliging, the Great Spirit turned him inside out and threw him in the river.

Love,

Leslie

21 May 1990

Dear Leslie,

French gardening is thriving and blossoming. In fact, after a three-day trip to Paris I am still in shock at the enthusiasm and effusiveness of *Ses Horticulturistes*. I had to go to do a talk about shrubs at a chateau called Courson about twenty-five miles south of Paris. Martyn, my co-author, went with me. (Martyn is a fantastic botanist who loves most of all searching the mountains of China or Africa or wherever for rare, new or lost plants in the grand manner of the old plant hunters.) Anyway, our French publishers, Flammarion, put us up in the Hotel Trianon on the Left Bank about three metres from the 'Boule Miche'. I was in slight trepidation of the hotel as years ago I stayed in the Hotel Petit Trianon on the Left Bank, which was incredibly cheap and incredibly itchy – the walls of the entire room were covered in squashed fleas and bugs!

The flower show was terrific. There is a whole new generation of French plantsmen; young, vital, keen and most of them specializing in one area of rarities or another. Of course lots of southern tender plants (I bought three Bougainvillea to see if I can get them to grow outside); but also I met a world expert on Japanese maples, a man with hundreds of carnivorous plants, a man with ancient roses, a man with more than two hundred different scented geraniums (not pelargoniums) and there were also lots of daturas. Then I met a man from Vallauris, where Picasso lived, who gave me some super things to pop in the garden – all incredibly tender. There was an artist who had made the most fantastic pots I have ever seen – very large terracotta and decorated all over with patterns in relief that reminded me of Arab jewellery. They cost about £700 each! so I didn't actually bring one home.

The next day I went to see the recreation of the Claude Monet garden at Giverny. About 10,000 other people had the same idea, but it is such a special place for me that I was able to walk around without even noticing them. Years ago I did some experimental photographs in different light, i.e. shots of the same view every hour from dawn to night. The changes were amazing and it showed how accurate Monet was in his subtle observation of light and colour. I think it would make a super project to go back to Monet's garden (on the closed day) and try to make a series of studies in different light.

After Monet we went on to a garden in a little valley near Dieppe, the 'Parc Floral des Moutiers'. The house is by E. L. Lutyens and Gertrude Jekyll acted as consultant on the garden, but I gather that her plans have become too expensive to keep up. As you approach the house there is a series of garden rooms divided up with lovely walls so that they continue the architecture of the house into the garden, thus making a natural transition between the architecture and the wooded garden that runs down to the sea. The point of all this is that one of the rooms is a white garden; and thinking of the articles you spoke of that you might have to do, I have done you a few photographs. The problem was that the garden was packed with visitors. There is a view showing the walls and arches that lead through from room to room: the walls have *Hydrangea petiolaris* and on the house, a climbing rose, and in the beds there are your favourite 'Iceberg' roses and masses of *Centranthus ruber* 'Albus'. I also enclose one shot taken down the valley from the house where wonderful rhododendrons were planted by the grandfather of the present family. As you look out from the terrace at the back of the house you see only lawns and woodland falling away down to the sea but hidden in the woodland are magnificent forty-foot-high rhododendron specimens planted in vast groups.

11 July

Back to 'Blighty' and the Square. Your (I think of them as 'your') Californian poppies are fantastic in different spots all around the garden. I have all the different colours I could get, but I think in the end I prefer the yellowy-orange and the reddish-orange – they look more natural. I have another great self-seeder packing out the spaces, and sometimes burying the camellias *Chelidonium majus* the greater celandine. Although it's very different from the California poppies they are closely related, it also makes a mass of blue-grey foliage. The genus is known for the bright orange latex that bursts out of every stem as you break it – just like a *Lactarius deliciosus* – but the whole plant is poisonous. It was an old cure for warts though – not eating it, that would be too permanent – just rubbing the 'milk' on them. Jean Palaisul wrote in his book *Grandmother's Secrets*: 'He who carries it (greater celandine) upon his person together with the heart of a mole will vanquish his enemies and win law suits.' Very useful in America that would be. The other well known use for the red milk is as a reviver of flagging sexual capabilities – how administered I leave to your imagination.

My *Rosa* Nevada are flowering like mad again. Looking back in my diary I find that they were at their height around 17 May. Do you grow it? Do you like it?

I had a letter from Rod Tulloss, the Amanita man. Apparently there were two bad poisonings in New England last season and he had been trying to identify the mushroom. After months of work he was able to prove that it was

Amanita
crenulata

Amanita crenulata described by Peck. – I had photographs of two collections that I had made in the Eastern states over the years but of course I could put no name to them. The information arrived from Rod the day I had to send the proofs of my mushroom book back so I was able to crush it in. I think it will be the first time a photograph of it has ever been printed.

No we don't have raccoons in London, or England for that matter. They look sweet but they sound like a disaster – everything in my garden lives on bonemeal so please don't send me a sweet little raccoon pup? kitten? calf? My worst pests this year are snails. They are having a field day amongst the hostas and ligularias that are supposed to give foliage variety to the fern bed.

I planted a few seeds years ago of a thing I was told was Crispy mallow, *Malva crispa*. As far as I can now ascertain in my reference works it is now a variety of *Malva verticillata*. Well, whatever the botanists decide its name is it's good to eat! It's used in an Egyptian dish, melokia soup, flavoured with ground coriander and cayenne, pepper and salt.

I have loads of it in the garden now and I think the only way I can keep it from taking over is to eat it. I forgot to look up the real recipe so I made up a soup. I cooked three cloves of chopped garlic in olive oil and added it to three potatoes and three big handfuls of mallow leaves that had been boiled for three-quarters of an hour in a weak chicken stock. I flavoured it with salt and pepper and then liquidized it in the wizzer. The mallow leaves have a mucilaginous quality which thickens the soup very nicely. The children were crazy about it.

Off to Cornwall for one week tomorrow – all rocky cliffs and big waves and lovely gardens full of blue hydrangeas. Write *soon*. Love,

Roger

Cushing, Maine

Well Roger you tease! All this about the flea-bitten Petit Trianon and your understandable trepidations and then zip about the Trianon proper. Was it Grand I hope? Must say one of the nice things about my extremely *petit* celebrity is the occasional opportunity to stay in nice hotels on somebody else's nickel. When I go to Philadelphia to do the Book and Cook celebration they put me up at the Four Seasons which is very *grand luxe* (as America goes), and even though I get the low end of what's available the rooms are nevertheless always the sort of rooms where I feel a bit abashed as I put my ratty old nightie in the *très élégant* bureau. Life in the lane of the expense account – it's all business travellers natch, deducting their brains out; but I don't think I'd better get involved in politics just now.

Come to think of it, those travellers may not be entirely fixed on business if the interesting discovery I made during my last stay is any indication. I was lying on the floor next to the bed, getting ready to do the assorted exercises that help to keep vastness at bay. Happened to turn my head and look under the bed and there was a pair of extremely scanty scanties – black, with lace. I suppose I should have turned them in to housekeeping, in case they had sentimental value for somebody or were perhaps immensely expensive designer scanties or something but instead I kept 'em (though I haven't yet found any occasion suitable for their display).

To return to your letter: Those young vital keen plantsmen (and women?) and the conference itself sound very stimulating. Frustrating, though, for those of us for whom bougainvillea is strictly the stuff of fantasy. Are you sure those scented geraniums aren't pelargoniums? I ask because I have a fancy geranium catalogue (Shady Hill Gardens, 821 Walnut Street, Batavia, Illinois 60510) that lists over a thousand varieties, seventy of them scented, and they're *all* pelargoniums of one sort or another. Can't say I'm much tempted by any of them, though 'Banded coconut' (*P. patulum*) sounds kind of engaging: 'white flower, coconut scent, rounded, pale green leaf with distinct zone; trailing.' Oh well, can't buy everything ... Please tell more about the daturas, I think they may have possibilities here – at least more possibilities than bougainvillea. My *D. suaveolens* of course failed to germinate; all I've got again this year is plain old jimson weed (*D. stramonium*), known as 'stinkweed' for very good reason. (I keep thinking I've got it extirpated but I keep being wrong.) *But*, my neighbor has something else, she knows not what – it's a very handsome low bush, the leaves gorgeous and trumpets immense, but it doesn't seem to be fragrant – and last spring I noticed some yet-another-kind being started by a local professional; so the genus (I notice on looking it up there are a *lot* of species) must offer a fair amount that would survive this far North.

The white garden you describe sounds glorious beyond words – can't wait to see the photos and am meanwhile reminded of so many things, among them a garden up north of here (near Bar Harbor) that was designed by Beatrix Ferrand. Lawns leading down a gentle slope to the sea have been planted with wild rose (*rugosa*, actually) hedges that look very natural but were actually carefully placed to enhance the perspective, making the sweep look far longer than it is. This architectural element is all that's left of the original, in all probability because this garden too was too expensive to keep up. Another aspect of the ephemerality that is such an essential part of gardening, for good or ill. Even Gertrude Jekyll's work not immune! This should point up the importance of learning to make those charts and diagrams as descriptive as possible, but there's still a bit of nagging doubt. You do say –

or did you? – that you feel Monet in his garden. The restoration there *sounds* very successful yet I wonder. Without the guiding spirit of the original designer, how can the caretakers/recreators copy or cope with the inevitable glitches and splendid surprises? What did Monet do when the snails wasted his clematis and he had to stick something else in the hole, quick?

At least with him we have the paintings. Much better than diagrams, apropos of which I must tell you mine of the yellow border is already inaccurate. Once the heliopsis started blooming they turned out to be all wrong – *way* too orange – and I had to get them out right away. Or sort of right away. They announced their unsuitability at the start of a killer dry heat wave and I had to keep patiently making bouquets with the about-to-open buds until the weather finally broke. They've settled in happily between a big bunch of very tall goldenglow and some squatty but indomitable *coreopsis* 'Early Sunrise' at the edge of the vegetable patch, where the three make a satisfying sweep of gold that leads the eye right to the edge of the woods (where it stops dead and blinks in disappointment. Design improvement there is definitely called for, a project for the fall).

I love *Hydrangea petiolaris* and it had been neck and neck with Dutchman's pipe (*Aristolochia durior*) for the place upon the wall where I need a vine and then I'd just about decided against (it takes quite a while to get established here and I need a more immediate show) when you bring the whole thing up again.

Don't know *Rosa* Nevada at all – looked it up in *Roses* where it doesn't seem to be listed in the index and went thence to Beales, where I saw a very nice picture and read on the same page 'Given the choice I would never exchange one bloom of Mme Hardy for an armful of Iceberg.' He goes on to add: 'Nor would I plant a bed of Mme Hardy in the middle of my lawn.' Reminds me that I really must get some of

Madame, no matter how hard it is to figure out where to put her, and how is one to make the garden smaller, hence more manageable and less full of weeds and generally lovelier and more civilized, if there is all this stuff one keeps wanting to plant?

And how, when it comes to roses, is one to be noble in the matter of the environment when one is plagued with thrips? Even assuming one had the time and it was environmentally wise to apply rotenone daily, it wouldn't work. Neither does insecticidal soap, garlic, sabadilla dust (which is in any case hell on the bees) . . . Organic gardening manuals inevitably advise you to plant resistant varieties when all else fails, but they never talk about how the things you *want* are always the most vulnerable. This year I was sent a sample of something called (approximately) 'Meidiland everblooming carefree landscape rose' which indeed it seems to be, big clusters of faintly fragrant little very double flowers and nice dark green leathery foliage on a good sized, spreading, healthy plant apparently unbothered by thrips, blackspot or the evil birch leaf miners that drop from above and devastate all other roses in the vicinity. But is it lovely? Is it noble, graceful, poignant, *interesting*? It is not. Pretty is about the kindest thing I can think of to say, damning with faint praise when you're talking about a rose.

August 10 . . . Already, so I think I'd better get this in the mail, although there's much else to tell and I will any day now. Do want you to know the photography is finally underway. I got the camera about two weeks ago, have used some film and am having a dandy time. After years and years of asking photographer friends, 'Please, would you memorialize this totally weird eggplant for me?' and 'Could you get a shot of the hollyhock – the way the light is coming through that petal?' etc., it's a great relief to finally be doing it (or at least trying to do it) myself. Still very frustrating as I don't yet know what the hell I'm doing, which is to say don't know how to set the images I see in the garden on the film. With my naked li'l eyeballs, for instance, I see quite clearly the way some pink *Limonium suworowii*, serendipitously planted beneath a group of common foxgloves (*D. purpurea*), echo not only their eccentric arches but also the tone, in a different shade, of their rather plummy color. *However*, getting this amusing juxtaposition nicely framed, correctly lighted, properly exposed, etc., has so far eluded me. I *see* a patterned tangle of spires in multiple, subtly various pinks, unified by a broad band of bright green leaf, but I seem to be photographing something between a bunch of pink moosh and the very worst sort of seed-catalogue illustration. Oh well, 'perseverance furthers', as an old I-ching-enamored friend used often to say. And as another friend has turned me on to a much less expensive film-processor than the one I started out with, your seed money should go a bit farther.

It does go, though, doesn't it? The old saw around here is that 'a sailboat is a hole in the water into which one pours money'. I think the same could be said of the garden excepting it's a hole in the ground and you have to dig the damn thing before you can pour the money into it.

More soon,

Leslie

Cushing, Maine

Dear Roger,

Just gave a little talk at the local historical society, title: 'Ecology in the Kitchen', a benefit for the Cushing Recycling Project. We're working on getting teaching materials for our school and a few neighboring ones, and the committee has decided to buy special bins – one for each of Cushing's roughly six hundred households – to make it easy to set out glass, plastic, etc. for the garbage man to collect as part of his regular rounds.

Our town landfill is now closed and you must drive about fifty miles round trip if you want to discard-your-own without paying a fee. A big change from when I first came here, and I rather miss Sunday At The Dump, a congenial source of local news and gossip if a bit gamey fragrance-wise, but the new regime has been very instructive. Now that we have to pay attention to where the trash goes we can really see where it comes from. In our case, it comes from the mailbox. We use very little packaged or canned food, the garden debris and kitchen scraps are composted, beer bottles are returnable and newspapers are used as mulch. What's left? Wine bottles and junk mail, roughly 450,000 times more of the latter than the former.

So, in keeping with the general theme I talked a lot about using leftovers, storing same in glass refrigerator containers or old yogurt tubs, composting – and eating weeds. Big hit. Almost all in the audience are country dwellers and most had heard of dandelions, but lamb's quarters, pigweed, purslane, the usual lot, turned out to be revelation. I passed around a bunch of lamb's quarters and purslane for tasting and the best

part was seeing the converts work on convincing the reluc-
tant. Now, if they all just go out and tell their friends.

Weeds in my opinion don't get nearly enough respect and
neither does the accidental landscape. We have for instance a
whole field of milkweed between the so-called orchard and
Lois's barn. It was in full perfection the middle two weeks of
July: fragrance to beat any jasmine and in the butterfly blue
twilight a multitude of fireflies to replace the monarchs of
afternoon. I suppose that's the ultimately comforting thing
about life in the country – most of its greatest delights do not
come (except inadvertently) from the hand of man.

Respect notwithstanding, I've had a hard time restraining
myself from weeding out all the purslane. Had to pay special
attention to be sure there'd be enough for the talk. Usually
there's plenty no matter how hard I try but this has been a
good year for tidiness on account of it's so dry that anything
weeded *stays* weeded. The problem is compounded because I
seem to have cleverly planted my garden in a drought pocket.
On more than one occasion it has remained rainless here
when it was pouring a mile down the road. The soil, as I have
probably already complained, is sandy, and to top it all off (or
not top it all off) I have a dug well only eleven feet deep. The
water is pretty much all for the garden but even all is not
enough.

Not my idea of a good time, but this is the plot I'm
allotted, and over the years I've learned a lot, duress the
teacher, about xeriscaping (our current vogue term for
designing gardens that use minimal added water). The grey-
leaved plants, especially the needle-leaved ones, really are
much more drought-tolerant. I'm appending a list, though
don't know how much good it'll do. I've also learned a bit
about rationing: to water the potatoes when they first set
flowers, the peas when the flowers are in bud, then again
when the pods start to fill. And tomatoes produce very tasty

fruit when the plants are a little bit stressed. The skins are on the tough side, but that isn't too big a deal. Same goes for peppers – in fact I think many fruiting plants produce better when not too lush and green.

Not too lush and green won't do this year, unfortunately, because the garden is about to be infested with photographers. I'm doing summer entertaining pieces for *Metropolitan Home* and *New York Times* magazines, pieces that will have Eating From (and In) the Garden as their themes. Both shoots are scheduled for early September so I'm madly mulching, praying and washing everything up to and including my teeth over at Lo's, so as to save every drop of water for the garden.

Which is looking pretty good as a result, rainlessness not-withstanding. Old dry gardener's tricks like setting out baby plants in little water-catching bowls scooped from the soil (and of course heavy reliance on mulch) are paying off. But things still look a little less full than they do in damper years, especially since around here you can't cram things in the way you could in a drier climate. How can we have drought and damp at the same time? Being English you will know the answer is Fog. Every third summer or so we get wall-to-wall fog for weeks on end and the mildew reaches epic propor-tions. Or would if permitted. So I keep the perennials at arm's length from each other and let the annuals fill in more or less each summer, depending on conditions.

What I do about the lawn is nothing and this year I'm paying the price. I have what's called a yachtsman's lawn – 'he mows what grows' – so it's always a bit discouraged by summer's end, more like an advertisement for clover than a rolling greensward. But this year *Ugh!* and I've got about two weeks to make it look like something you'd want to have a romantic picnic on. We have had one big thundershower (just the other day), but that's the classic day late and a dollar short. Lawn paint (yes, Roger, there really is such a thing, which its seller proudly claims is 'lifelike' and non-toxic to plants or people) is out of the question so I think I'll just spread a number of Persian rugs and runners over the offending stubble and hope it looks artistic.

The food I feel more confident about. Heavy on the gorgeous vegetables. I'm planning a large plate of sliced tomatoes, showing off the colors of 'White Beauty', 'Lemon Boy' (hideous name but a fine bright yellow and very nicely balanced flavor), 'Evergreen' (thick-skinned but very sweet as it turns out and 'Nepal' (have I mentioned it? bright red slicers, not too large, good true tomato flavor and breathtaking uniformity for an open-pollinated fruit, each one baseball size and shape, big red peas in a pod).

Also a similarly colorful assortment of potatoes, simply steamed, partially peeled and piled in a shallow basket. 'All Blue', actually a fine deep violet, 'German Lady Fingers', which are a pale primrose yellow inside; 'Red Gold', the inside of which is a deep gold; 'Caribe' for its very white flesh. I may throw a few beets in here too, haven't made up my mind. The hot item in that department is 'Chioggia', candy-striped red and white and offered by more and more chic catalogues as 'an old Italian variety'. They really are lovely, though not too much to write home (or to Roger) about in the taste department. And you have to serve them raw if you want to preserve the color. *But* the color really is spectacular. So far the best thing I know to do is to slice them very thin, like chips, and serve them with dips the same way.

There will be lots of thick green herbal sauces, natch. Basil is one place I have put the water and although the coriander has of course bolted in the heat, I'm planning to wow the folks by sprinkling the fish with soft green coriander seeds. They're delicious. Not sold in stores. Same like radish pods and rocket flowers. In the U.S., by the way, nobody knows what you're talking about when you say rocket. You have to call it *arugula* since only Italian communities have had anything to do with it for about the last century. Funny to wonder how this and other old English herbs, so popular with the colonists, seem to have vanished until just a few years ago – lovage, burnet, chamomile, tansy. Well, they're coming back now.

And I'm going – to deadhead what is this year a positive sea of white cosmos. It's very impressive at the moment and I want it to keep on plugging until the photographers come. After that, the goldfinches can have their field day eating the seeds. I intend to let the garden hang and go mushrooming instead.

Love,

Leslie

Garden plants that have done well in Cushing garden when rainfall was below average

Achillea – all varieties except *A. ptarmica*
Armeria maritima
Artemesia – all except *lactiflora*
Calliopsis
Coreopsis – *grandiflora* does better than *verticillata*
Centaurea cyanus
Cerastium tomentosum
Convolvulus (Ipomoea) purpurea
Eschscholzia Californicum
Gazania rigens
Hemerocallis – the 'wild' orange (*H. fulva*) types do better than the fancy
  hybrids
Lavendula augustifolia
Liatris spicata
Limonium latifolium
Nicotiana affinis
Oenothera missouriensis
Oreganum vulgare
Papaver – all varieties, esp. *P. rhoeas* and *P. somniferum*
Portulaca grandiflora
Rosa Rugosa – depends. 'Blanc double de Coubert' languishes. Lois's
  nameless magenta ('Roseraie de l'Hay'?) is unfazed

Rosmarinus officinalis
Ruta graveolens
Salvia – most varieties both culinary and ornamental but not *patens*
Santolina chamaecyparissus
Senecio cineraria
Thymus – every blessed one I've ever grown has been very drought-tolerant
Tropaeolum majus
Yucca filamentosa
Zinnia haageana

VEGETABLES: Forget it, except melons which taste better if not watered once fruit has sized up. Best seed source for drought-tolerant vegetable varieties is Native Seeds/SEARCH, a non-profit organization dedicated to preserving the Native American agriculture of the Southwest, 2509 N. Campbell Ave. #325, Tucson, AZ U.S.A. 85719

Garden plants commonly recommended as drought-tolerant that have not proved noteworthily so in Cushing garden

Cleome hasslerana
Cosmos bipinnatus
Echinops ritro
Helianthus annuus
Stachys byzantina (lanata)
Tagetes erecta, T. patula. T. tenuifolia does OK but still not great
Verbena rigida
Zinnia augustifolia

29 August 1990

Dear Leslie,

We have been having temperatures here that I associate with Florida or Texas; about two weeks ago it was up in the high nineties with an all time record of 98.5°F. A friend recorded 105°F in the shade in his garden on that day. I picked that day to go off to the south of France where it was even hotter. But the vineyards were in fine shape and I expect it will be a good year for French wines although the droughts that they have had will no doubt mean a small crop. Virtually the only other plant showing any sign of life in France was your jimson weed, *Datura stramonium* (we usually call it thorn apple because of its horribly thorny fruits). This grew in profusion all around the converted barn we had rented for our trip, though it had some assistance: every evening just at dusk when we were playing *Boules*, the 'Gardener' Gerard would arrive to water. He watered the lavender and the hedge that had been planted to shield the pool from the enquiring eyes of the passers-by – totally ineffectual as any full blooded Frenchman or woman will stop the car and get out for a good substantial stare – and after the new hedge he then watered the jimson weed. The result, as you can imagine, a stinking forest.

The aubergines looked so good in the markets I thought I must have a go at a dish that I ate in Paris about a hundred years ago. A friend of mine from school, Ann Wigzell, married a French actor called Grégoire 'Coco' Aslan. Actually he was an Armenian. His mother was a terrific cook and she made us this very simple but most wonderful Armenian aubergine dish. I think the proper name for it is caviare d'aubergine. I allowed one large aubergine per person. Burn the aubergine skins over a naked flame and peel them, slice them and liberally salt them leaving for a few hours to sweat. Wipe off most of the salt and fry in really good, first-pressing olive oil for about ten minutes until absolutely soft. Take off the heat and squeeze over it a liberal amount of fresh garlic, tip the whole lot into a flat dish and mash it all up together. Fork over the surface and then leave it to go cold. It sounds so simple yet all the flavours – the oil, the salt, the burnt surface of the aubergine and the quarter-cooked garlic – are a perfect combination.

Coco was a fascinating man who told super stories of the great French beauties like Bardot and Mylene Demongeot, but what interested me most was that he had started his career as a swing drummer. Years later I was listening to a record programme and the disc jockey played a record by Roger Roger et son Orchestre featuring dans les batteries the great 'Coco' Aslan.

Back to daturas. My big tree one has failed to flower again this year so I still don't know what it is. Three years ago a plant of belladonna, *Atropa belladonna* appeared in the garden and I encouraged it for its lovely purple bell flowers and terrific shiny fruit. It was a mistake. This year I have young plants all over the garden. What I have succeeded in doing is finding the most fecund weed of summer. I must have pulled out over a hundred already. The rate of growth is incredible; it seems to be about fifteen inches high in a week and also to come into flower that quickly. I have decided to keep the original plant. It is well tucked away from children's prying hands, as it's so poisonous. Each year I will cut it back before the birds start to eat the berries – if I remember.

The Society for the Protection of London Squares is developing apace. I have had to research the history and legal aspect of squares and this led me to a fascinating book called *Report on London Squares* by the Royal Commission of 1928, a gigantic work which led to an Act of Parliament in 1931. It is a most thorough work with details of 461 London squares telling you who owned them, what the condition of the garden was, how they were financed, etc. I am now attempting to re-examine all the squares to see what has happened in the meantime and what the modern problems of financing them and, of course, protecting them, might be. A gigantic task: so far I am in contact with about fifty or sixty squares and am in the process of getting details out of the various garden committees. We had a drinks evening in Eccleston Square and about a hundred turned up. It was fascinating to hear of all their problems. One square has only the legal right to charge £1 per house per annum garden rate. This generates £37 a year, enough for one gardener for one day a year! One of the techniques of the developers is to buy a block of houses together and then leave them to fall to bits. After five or ten years of neglect the damage is terrific, so they go to the local planning authority and propose to turn the whole site into offices or a hotel or whatever. The planning authority normally tells them that they must remain as private houses whereupon the developer says that the cost of repairing them would be greater than any possible income he might gain. Then the whole thing is left and the buildings degenerate and degenerate. Next time round the developer puts up a new plan, perhaps with some sweetener involved, and so it goes until he gets his way, unless the residents stay diligent and keep up their objections.

We have these marvellous green areas in our city that make it human and liveable in. It is ergo the actual inhabitants who must fight for every square foot that is left. The office worker or even the hotel visitor looks for convenience in the short term and might well support developers trying to build car parks or whatever. This means that we have to fight the incursion of businesses into the private houses of the squares. The other awful prospect is that any city planner wandering around looking for sites for amenities like electrical, gas or water substations or new underground railways buildings naturally first looks at the open spaces – the poor old squares, again. At the moment there is a plan to build a new underground railway building on Parliament Square right opposite the House of Commons. The rotting houses ploy seems to be in practice in Stanhope Gardens, a lovely large square which has derelict houses on two complete sides and is causing horrible problems for the remaining residents.

My historical research on our square has also been fascinating. Pimlico (our district) is a triangle about one mile by one mile by one mile bordered on the south by the River Thames. Up to 1828 the majority of it was a market garden which grew vegetables for London. The land was incredibly fertile, giving three or even four crops of vegetables a year, first peas then turnips then potatoes then cabbages. Our little corner did not in fact grow vegetables but was part of a reservoir system that supplied water to London as it then was. This consisted of a wonderfully balanced ecological system of allowing the incoming salt tide on the river to push the down-flowing fresh water up into the reservoir system and at the same time use the weight of water to drive a massive wooden pumping system which lifted the water to an even higher level so that there was a head of water to service the customers who lived at a slightly higher level. The pumping engine was a marvel of its time and was visited by the elegant ladies of the late eighteenth century. The main reservoir area is now Victoria Station and the canals that fed it provided the land to build the railway tracks out to the river – then over it and on south.

One of the other elements of this water system was an area of tiny canals about twenty feet apart into which the new water from the river was run to let it settle and clarify.

Between and around these mini-canals were planted willows or more specifically sallows to grow the 'withes' to make the baskets for the vegetables grown on the rest of the Pimlico area. Eccleston Square is on the site of these canals and 'withe' beds. So my latest project is to have a small demonstration bed of sallows in the garden. I have spoken to the chief dendrologist (tree historian) at the Forestry Commission and he is looking into the plant history of the area to see if he can find exactly which of the hundreds of forms, hybrids, cultivars or whatever would have been the ones originally grown.

In reply to your letter, the geraniums that I referred to are pelargoniums; not geraniums in the botanical sense but of course in the vernacular both are geraniums. Have you seen the new book *Index Hortensis* by Piers Trehane? It is referred to as the authoritative guide to the correct naming of perennial plants (more volumes may follow eventually). It has become our bible. Trehane lists 152 geraniums proper many of which are just cultivars. Pelargoniums he doesn't list as they fit into the tender or bedding plant category, but as you say there are at least 1000 different cultivars in commerce.

I misled you a bit over *Rosa* Nevada – it is not a species and should therefore not be *Rosa* Nevada but just the Rose Nevada. A pedantic point but if you now look it up in our *Roses* book you will find two pictures of it (p. 104/5) – one a lovely specimen at the Savill Gardens in Windsor Great Park. My plants still have quite a lot of flowers, it's such a wonderful vigorous thing, I feel reasonably sure that it would be hardy in Maine.

They have plants of it at Pickering Nurseries Inc., 670 Kingston Road, Hwy 2, Pickering, Ontario, and also at Historical Roses, 1657 West Jackson Street, Painsville, OH 44077.

As far as the photography is concerned, keep at it, and then keep at it again. Remember you need constant practice to keep your hand in.

I am still grappling with understanding your complaints about the woman who wandered into your garden. On a fine day we often have as many as a hundred people in the square garden. Privacy is at a minimum but lots of opportunities for chats. What we don't have we don't miss!

Love,

Roger

Cushing, Maine

Dear Roger,

Your letter was a delight and will be answered . . . not right this minute. Another major food shoot in the garden tomorrow and the next day, book MSS overdue back at the copy editor's *already* and . . .

Yours in haste,

Leslie

Cushing, Maine

Dear Roger,

Your letter proper is still in process but I wanted to get these photos to you so you could critique them before I do the potatoes and beets. I'll be doing the peppers while these are in transit but might be able to redo them if I heard from you soon enough, so please call if these are all wrong. I've already noticed that doing everything with the same background may not be such a bright idea and will seek others that are similarly unobtrusive – it ain't easy!

And neither is getting the color right. Most of the stuff was done with Ektachrome 100, which seems to make everything a bit yellower than it should be (cloudy days or shadowy places employed almost throughout, by the way). Fuji 50 on the brandywines doesn't seem to have helped; they're still the wrong color. Can this be fixed in the printing? Should I be using some kind of filter?

Still too much to do. Such as be inspired by your historical delving into the London squares. It made me wonder as I did when I first came about the history of this place. Cushing itself is fairly old as U.S. settlements go; we had our bicentennial two years ago, I think it was. As far as this specific plot is concerned I know almost nothing except that the potato farm would have been in the 1920s or 30s.

Cushing has always been primarily a fishing village – it's all lobsters now – and I do know there was a clam factory (actually a processing plant where the clams were shucked and packed) about three thousand feet from here as the crow flies, on a spit of land above the river. The factory and the farm that followed it are now gone, the land strewn with modern houses. But I've seen a photo of the factory workroom, taken in 1903, that shows long trestle tables piled with clams. There are about a dozen women in whaleboned shirtwaists and long skirts, most of them seated at the tables. Their hands are temporarily idle, they are valiantly facing the camera. I have been told they came to work from all over Cushing and also, in rowboats, from Tenants Harbor across the river.

I know the main road to the point used to run right through the field that is now our orchard. It ran on a diagonal down the hill and by the creek below the lower garden. When the state paved and widened the way they moved the road to its present location on the northwest side of the property. You can still see the track of the old road, in part because I occasionally drive down it in the truck, to bring manure to the lower garden.

Your eggplant dish sounds delicious, *baba ghanouj* without the complication of *tahini*. I make similar dishes all fall; eggplants take a long time here but when they start producing they come all at once and you have to think up ways to eat lots. I used to put them up by making *caponata*, doing it the old-fashioned way, individually deep-frying in olive oil first the celery, then the onions, then the salted and drained eggplant, *then* simmering everything a good long time in a spicy, thick, sweet and sour tomato sauce. The result is canned and is, as they say, of long conservation, a dark, intense, velvety sort of eggplant jam for which I was (if I say it myself) locally famous. It has been some time since I made any because each year I try another short-cut in hopes of finding a modification tasty enough yet mainstream enough to be put in a column. Alas, all of the short-cuts are dross compared to the labor-intensive real thing.

A lesson there, but we knew that. Stay well.

October 21 1990

Last night was the night of doom. Today it's all black frost under the still-flaming leaves, an abrupt end to all but the hardiest. Usually I've got everything covered but this year has been just too topsy turvy and to tell the truth I'm glad. When I first started gardening in Maine, there was always frost in early September and serious cold by October, but the last few years have had long slow warm falls, and I have had squash plants that died of old age, ancient annuals that dropped with exhaustion, a garden that ungracefully decayed instead of getting slammed while still in vigorous bloom. No question I've gotten higher yield and at least six more weeks of cut flowers, but at a considerable price.

What I like, I've decided, is sudden early death, the kind of frost that brings sight of the end while there's still plenty of blue sky and crisp apple left to enjoy. I want to clip off all the old stalks, weed out what I can and move a few delphiniums around while the sun is still strong enough so you can work in thin summer clothing. I really like cleaning up a lot better than planting. All that spent stuff piled on the compost, the soil – or at least patches of it – smoothly dark brown. The raised beds once more almost formal in their rectangular geometry.

Finally (for about five minutes) I can *see* the garden whole. It's the history of art all over again. A suffocating Victorian jungle of overgrown summer is swept away into smooth earth. Weed-free, indeed very nearly plant-free, it's like the fresh breath of modernism, the recurring triumph of struc-ture over detail.

There's also, of course, a very agreeable sense of comple-tion. When all the potatoes are in the cellar, the leeks and swiss chard hilled with straw. When all the bulbs are planted, all the tools cleaned, when the garden is hidden by the all-forgiving snow, I get a chance to lie fallow myself for a while, resting body and mind before the growth cycle starts again. You, on the other hand, have something happening in the garden all year round, which at this point in my life I'm no longer sure is a blessing.

Cushing, Maine

Dear Roger,

The hard frost on October 20 was a real whammer – it probably went down to around 28 and stayed there for several hours – so only a few of the hardiest things are left. Calendula endures, of course, there's still a pansy or two here and there, and second-crop spires of delphinium, along with a very pretty slightly lavendered-blue annual salvia (*S. farinacea*, 'Blue Bedder') that's turning out to be unexpectedly tough. Leeks are doing fine, also the chard, carrots, beets, lettuces and a gratifying plenitude of rocket. The parsley all bolted long ago; perhaps because of drought, perhaps because I was so slow planting it out that it got disgustingly potbound.

Each day as I walk over to the mailbox (I'm still in the summer house) I think, well, time to make the annual diagram of what went where (the one I should have done in midsummer) so I can yank up the assorted corpses and do some planting before the ground freezes. But what with this and what with that I have of course done nothing and the giant box of spring bulbs mocks me six or seven times a day. So do the little pots of *Onopordum*, which I can't quite decide where to put in view of those monster thorns. And there are all these tiger-lilies I want to move from the lower garden to the hot-color bed near the greenhouse. But the other day I *did* manage to do some seed gathering, feeling now or neverish since frost means rot, scattering, and the attentions of the birds. Late fall now, the trees mostly unleafed and it's getting brisk, but seed day was sunny and blue, warm enough to go jacketless. It's a fussy job but I love the architecture of the pods. What a fine collection of cunning boxes they are.

This year's revelation in the seedcase department was the portulaca, which I've never collected before. At the end of each stem is a cluster of shallow cups, each with a perfect onion dome lid, each filled brimming with tiny seeds. Did it this year as the variety, 'Swan Lake', was both extraordinarily lovely (a pure but soft white) and extraordinarily expensive. Might as well give it a go, though I hope I can get it going early enough so it starts blooming before transplanting time, in case I have to rogue out any throwbacks. Which will be throwbacks to what, I wonder. Will they be some kind of wishy-washy pink, like everything else in creation that isn't yellow? Never until this minute wondered what the wild form of portulaca looks like (the ice plant that grows wild on the coast of California blooms in cheap baby-blanket colors, gutless pink and blue), but purslane's white, as I remember it. I've put a lot of energy into removing the blinking purslane *before* it flowers – we mostly eat it in salad though Lois, who has a high slime-tolerance, likes it cooked, too – so I can't quite imagine the flowers at the moment.

Really cleaned up in the morning glories, trying to be sure of a good supply of one of this year's happiest finds, a deep royal purple variety called 'Kniola's Black', supposedly a wildling noticed and perpetuated by a farmer in Iowa. Regardless of origin it was splendid, rather smaller than the common Japanese type, with hairier vines and earlier, much more prolific bloom. Mixed with old standby 'Heavenly Blue' it made a splendid screen at the edge between the blue border and the white garden, so I tried to collect up enough to spread around by giving little packets to deserving friends for Christmas (do you want some?)

Love,

Leslie

4 December 1990

Dear Leslie,

God, it's months since I wrote. First the tomato photographs were superb. You put me to shame. They were so
good I felt like giving up! You ask about colour film Ektachrome 100 versus Fuji 50; there is no answer to the question
which is best. There are slight differences of emphasis – you
pays your money and takes your choice. Also film changes a
lot every time they make a new batch. The batch number is
overprinted on the box next to the use-by date. If you get a
roll you like the colour of, go back to the shop with the
number and buy all the rest of the stock they have.

Now to your second letter. Thanks for another set of
fantastic photographs, I am knocked out with the 'Yellow
Ruffled' tomato and especially the Hyacinth Bean which we
had tried to get hold of and failed. A couple of points on the
shots: focusing becomes a problem in two ways, one when
you shoot smaller objects and thus have to get in closer and
two, as the light gets weaker in the winter. There are two
solutions and by combining them you will be able to sort it
out.

(1) Make sure you do not need to focus from near the lens
to far away all in the same shot, by keeping the vegetables
nearly in the same plane rather than spread out away from the
camera. The depth of field is the area that is in focus as seen
from the camera – as the lens is opened up to compensate for
poor light it gets less and less.

(2) Do not let the camera's tiny mind think for itself; you
must use the manual override to make sure that the lens stops
down. Left to itself it will shoot at say f2.8 at 1/60 of a

second, but to get your depth of field you may need f16. This means setting the shutter speed at ½ second, and of course this means mounting the camera on a *firm* tripod.

Another critical element is deciding where to focus. Providing you are going to stop down at least 3–4 stops the place to focus is about a quarter of the way back from the front of the shot. This will then mean that the front vegetable and the back ones will pull into focus. If, however, you are not able to stop down – say you are hand holding the camera for some reason – then you must get the front vegetable in focus. It will look crummy if only one middle one is in focus. End of lecture. I hope I am not being too pedantic.

I told you about our Kemp leaf shredder – it really is a marvel, the ground-up leaves are halfway broken down in a couple of weeks. This year I am trying to a new ploy; where we have cleared out old shrubs and are putting in a new planting, once the shrubs and bulbs (if any) are in I am putting a 6″–8″ layer of the two week old half-rotted leaf choppings on to the bare earth. The idea is to keep the new shrubs a bit warm in the winter and then in the spring I hope it will keep back the weeds. Our worst offender is chickweed, it goes mad from the beginning of March onwards. I am also hoping that by April it will have started to rot well down, because I then plan to seed it with annuals which I am hoping will be able to germinate through the mulch. If it works it will be brilliant so cross your fingers for me. The only disadvantage is that if it does indeed hold back the weeds it will also hold back my self-seeding annuals. And so it goes.

Portulaca oleracea is India's contribution to the salad world – the flowers are yellow and about one-eighth of an inch across. In England they hardly ever come out as they need really bright sun – not like my beloved osteospermums that obediently open with good light rather than strong sun. Osteospermum has been a revelation in the garden over the last two hot summers, flowering from mid May to December. In

November I took loads of cuttings which I keep in a small tunnel made of bent bamboos covered in plastic, so if we do get a bad frost I should at least have new plants for next year.

Over the last few years I have been getting more and more interested in ceanothus. They do very well in London, they positively thrive on the drought and the summer heat we have been getting and they are hardy down to about 15°F below which we don't get (in ten years I haven't lost one.) The collection has now built up to thirty-six different entities, eleven species and twenty-five cultivated forms. We have an organization that has been set up to save garden plants called the National Council for the Conservation of Plants and Gardens. They have a scheme under which certain gardens hold what is called the 'National Collection'. There is already a National Collection of ceanothus at a place over near the west coast, Cannington, but the Council think it would be worth having another registered collection in London. I have talked to the people at Cannington and they have given me cuttings of all that they have that I don't (about twenty) and I have given them cuttings of all that I have that they don't (about two). When I have plants of all these I will have nearly sixty entities. Apart from these I have been in contact with two nurseries in California and am now attempting to get the customs clearance to bring to this country another twenty or so that can be found in the U.S.A. If I solve all this I then have to find room for eighty to ninety giant plants in the garden. I'm enclosing my current list. In England they are almost always grown as wall plants but this is only to give them winter protection – I have no walls so I grow them all free standing, or, as they are easily blown over, free propped would be nearer to the truth but nevertheless they grow in a much more natural way than up a wall.

Ceanothus Collection

Held at Eccleston Square Garden London S.W.1. Open twice a year under the National Garden Scheme or on application to: The Eccleston Square Garden Committee, c/o Roger Phillips, 15a Eccleston Square, London S.W.1. Tel: 071 834 8654

Plants are listed in alphabetical order, the key number in front of each plant is the number marked on the bed map of the garden, the number/s after each name tell you which of the beds it is planted in. Date of planting is in () approximate age at planting 1–2 years.

1. *C. americanus* 5 (1989)
42. *C. arboreus* 7 (1991)
25. *C. cyaneus* 7 (1990)
9. *C. dentatus* 6/17 (1990)
38. *C. dentatus* var. *floribundus* 17 (1990)
51. *C. divergens* 38 (1991)
11. *C. impressus* 6 (1989)
46. *C. incanus* 31 SICK (1991)
50. *C.* × *lobbianus* 38 (1991)
40. *C. maritimus* 24 (1991)
49. *C. megacarpus* 1 (1991)
53. *C. papillosus* 6 (1992)
24. *C. purpureus* 17 (1990)
29. *C. rigidus* var. *pallens* 15 (1990)
27. *C. spinosus* 31 (1990)
16. *C. thyrsiflorus* 1 (two)/5 (two)/13/28 (two) 30/32 (1982)
17. *C. thyrsiflorus* var. *repens* 35/41 (1986)
30. *C.* × *veitchianus* 36 (1990)
26. *C. verrucosus* 6 (1989)
3. *C.* 'Autumnal Blue' (*arboreus*) 16 (1990)
2. *C.* 'A. T. Johnson' 17 (1988)
23. *C.* 'Blue Cushion' 17 (1990)
4. *C.* 'Blue Mound' 5 (1987)
28. *C.* 'Brilliant' 15 (1991)
5. *C.* 'Burkwoodii' 5 /40 (1987)
41. *C.* 'Burtoniensis' 1 (1991)
6. *C.* 'Cascade' 35 (two)/36/37 (three) (1984)
22. *C.* 'Chelsea Blue' 17 (1990)
21. *C.* 'Concha' 17 (1990)
7. *C.* 'Delight' 5/40 (1987)
37. *C.* 'Dignity' 7 (1990)
44. *C.* 'Eleanor Taylor' 31 (1991)

35. C. 'Emily Brown' (*gloriosus*) 15 (1990)
43. C. 'Frosty Blue' 6 (1989)
 8. C. 'Gloire de Versailles' (× *delileanus*) 16 (1990)
10. C. 'Henri Desfosse' (× *delileanus*) 5 (1988)
34. C. 'Hurricane Point' (*griseus*) 17 (1990)
12. C. 'Italian Skies' 6 (1989)
36. C. 'Joyce Coulter' 15 (1990)
48. C. 'Louis Edmunds' (*griseus*) 17 1991
13. C. 'Marie Simon' (× *pallidus*) 37 (1989)
39. C. 'Mount Vision' 23 (1991)
14. C. 'Perle Rose' (× *pallidus*) 17 (1989)
15. C. 'Puget Blue' 32/37 (1986)
31. C. 'Sierra Blue' 15 (1990)
47. C. 'Sierra Snow' 7 (1991)
52. C. 'Snow Ball' (*rigidus*) 5 (1991)
45. C. 'Snow Flurries' (*thyrsiflorus*) 7(SICK)/13 (SICK) (1991)
32. C. 'Southmead' (× *lobbianus*) 17 (1990)
20. C. 'Thunder Cloud' 17 (1990)
18. C. 'Topaz' (× *delileanus*) 16 (1990)
19. C. 'Trewithen Blue' (*arboreus*) 5 (1987)
33. C. 'Yankee Point' (*griseus* var. *horizontalis*) 37 (1989)

BED 5
The Ceanothus Bed

BED 5: THE CEANOTHUS BED

All the areas between the plants are deeply mulched with bark and chopped-up leaves, giving the appearance of the floor of a dense beech wood. In the centre of the bed there is a small hidden area that the children who play in the garden can use as a secret camp. Also the cherry is a big strong tree with convenient low branches that we let the children climb.

SHRUBS

A = *Arundinaria murielae*
B = *Azalea* 'George Reynolds'
C = *Berberis darwinii*
D = *Ceanothus americanus*
E = *Ceanothus* 'Blue Mound'
F = *Ceanothus* 'Burkwoodii'
G = *Ceanothus* 'Delight'
H = *Ceanothus* 'Henri Desfosse'
HH = *Ceanothus rigidus* 'Snow Ball'
I = *Ceanothus thyrsiflorus*
J = *Ceanothus* 'Trewithen Blue'
K = *Chaenomeles japonica*
L = *Corylopsis sinensis*
M = *Cotoneaster salicifolius floccosus*
N = *Fatsia japonica*
O = *Halesia monticola*
P = *Ilex aquifolium*
PP = *Laburnum anagyroides*
Q = *Lavendula spica*
R = *Magnolia sinensis*
S = *Mahonia* 'Charity'
T = *Prunus* 'Kanzan'
U = *Pyracantha watereri*
UU = Rose Alchemist
W = *Rhododendron dauricum* 'Midwinter'
X = *Rhododendron* 'Pink Pearl'
Y = *Skimmia japonica*
Z = *Spirea thunbergii*

The rose 'Alchemist' (UU) sprawls all over the holly with stems well over twenty feet high, at least five feet higher than all the books say it should grow! Of all the roses we have in the garden it attracts the most attention with its very old-fashioned cabbagey flowers that change from having an orangey centre when they open to a pale gold centre as they mature – hence its name.

PERENNIALS

AA = Michaelmas daisy, some form or other of the *Aster nova-belgii*: only an ordinary bluish one but it makes a superb clump five feet round and four feet high, flowering from August to November.

BB = *Actea pachypoda*, the American woodland dolls eyes, but mine is a funny form of it that has a whole clump of eyes bunched together at the end of each of the little red stems rather than the normal one eye per stem.

CC = Hostas There are about ten rather large hosta plants along the front of the bed, all of them rather late flowering so that I get a good show from the end of July onwards.

Please write soon. Apart from your past life I need more ideas for interesting annuals, especially native American ones. Love,

Roger

Train to Poughkeepsie,
New York

Dear Roger,

I'm currently on the train – pardon attendant wiggles – travelling from New York to Poughkeepsie (two hours north–west in the Hudson River Valley). Outside, a grey landscape in fog: the river, lightly stippled, is the color of concrete. Every trackside tree, each weed, is glazed with ice, greyed with the glazing – in the distance the hills are as soft as spring. Occasionally the fog lifts and grey clouds move across the grey sky.

Bulletin: train has just passed a chain-link fenced hilltop – on the fence a sign: Fantasy acres/MUDBOG.

Not the most inspiring of landscapes, in spite of some noteworthy icicle formations. But I'm told the Hudson Valley is gorgeous; I'm primed for it to be so by famous paintings (the Hudson River School is enjoying a big revival here by the way) and, I suppose, it had better be, because I'm going to move here to make a partnered life with Bill Bakaitis.

You are perhaps not so surprised. I'm surprised, myself, and disinclined to make predictions about the success of the project, but so far so good. We moved to our present involvement from a phone + mail friendship that grew out of the Rindge mushroom foray. His long-suffering marriage came to an end last spring, when his wife asked for a divorce (not for the first time) and their mutual efforts to avoid that course were unavailing. He came for a clear-the-head-go-mushrooming and general R & R visit this last fall and here I am. I think. My head and most of my heart (the non-Bill part) are still in Maine, and I'll be going back mid-April or early May to get the garden in. Bill will join me for the summer (God Bless Teaching) and I guess from there we'll see.

Ducks taking off. Across the river, many mansions – and several fortress-like constructions that can't possibly *all* be prisons and hospitals but look like they should be.

January 15

Your letters – and my obligations – pile up apace. But as soon as I finish the seed orders you'll be hearing more . . . assuming, of course, that the world does not in one way or another come to an end (feeling very gloomy on that score and couldn't stop crying when the tanks rolled into Lithuania. Can't claim I was surprised; but I sure was sad.)
More soon,

Leslie xx

4 February 1991

Dear Leslie

When I heard your news all I could think to do was wander around the garden picking one of every flower that I could find. The pressed results (picture on back cover) are my best wishes for you – I hope it works out really well for both of you – I have known Bill since the New Jersey Mushroom foray in 1984!

No I am not really surprised. When no letter arrived through December I came to the conclusion you were dead or in love – the arrival of your letter told me you were alive.

I love-love-love your article on the garden; it sounds so enchanting I can't wait to see it, I hope when I get over to Maine in mid-August it will be at its best. Leslie, what a hard decision to make to leave your garden and half your heart in Cushing! I hope it works out that you can be a gardener half the year and a partner for the other half. Will this give you more time to write to me? I hope so. I'm sorry that I didn't thank you for *The New England Epicure*. I have been reading it over lunch, and I am up to Halloween. The chapter that knocked me out was when you had to cook a bath-long salmon and used the bath as a fish kettle by putting hot rocks into the water native-American style. I can't wait to try it, it's so simple, so obvious and I am sure so effective.

I am now fixing dates for my publicity launch for *Mushrooms of North America*. So far Boston is fixed for 16 May then 20 to 24 May the West Coast, Los Angeles, San Francisco, Seattle, Portland and across to Denver. I will be giving a lecture every night. My current plan is to mix up the slides every night and thus show them in different ways so that I don't start repeating myself and put the audience and myself to sleep.

Why don't you and Bill come over for a pseudo honeymoon? and I can take you on a grand tour of English gardens. I gather you can get round trips USA Europe for about $200. We will put you up. I am going to visit lots of historic gardens this year – I have decided that it is time I made a real study of gardening history. My plot is this year England (plus USA?) next year Italy, Spain and Portugal. To visit gardens in USA I need a really good book on your historic and important gardens. Is there such a book? Title, publisher, please.

This winter is much colder than last year and everything in the garden is much more behind – it's probably better. Last year on 2 February I had flowers on thirty different camellia plants, this year I have flowers on 5 and in fact only one flower on each. I keep telling everyone how much better it will be when the weather finally warms up as they will all flower at once and make a real show. (Maybe you should hop on a flight and get here for the first week of March.)

On 29 January we return willows to their home in our garden. John White (the dendrologist) has come up with a theory as to what plants may have been grown here. Amongst his collection of willows (he holds the National Collection of some hundreds of willows), is *Salix viminalis* from 'Little London', an area of market gardens and small holdings on the River Welland in Lincolnshire, about a hundred miles from London. I quote John's letter: 'It seems likely that market gardeners moved there from London in the nineteenth century (buildings do not pre-date 1850). This was probably associated with the extension of the London and North-Eastern Railway from Peterborough. This willow is unlike the local wild *Salix viminalis* so I suggest it is an Osier of London origin.'

We know that the lease on our land was obtained on Lady

The 'New-London'
Willow

Day 1828 and the developer, Thomas Cubitt, started to clear
out the market garden and willow growers from the area; it
must have taken some time as the reports talk of great battles
and problems getting them off the land. The first house
(number one) was completed by 1836, but then I gather there
was a property slump (nothing changes) so that by 1850 only
twenty-three houses had been completed. All this backs up
John's supposition and until further evidence comes to hand,

if it ever does, I am accepting 'Little London' as the best bet.

John White sent me cuttings with planting instructions. Willow cuttings by tradition must not be planted until after the first full moon in January. For sound reasons: if you plant them earlier the soil may be warm enough to cause them to strike – then the frosts of January and February push the cuttings upwards breaking off the juvenile roots. Leaving it until late January means that by the time the soil warms up and the little roots start to grow the chance of a severe frost is over. So, attended by a small group of garden lovers, the cuttings were duly planted and a small libation poured on to the soil, most of the libation descending down the throats of said garden lovers.

Lots of love and fun for you both.

Roger

P.S. Are you of Lithuanian descent?

Clinton Corners, New York

February 25 1991

Dear Roger,

More time to write? More time to write? *Ha*! Nevertheless, I will be in touch soon and am meanwhile utterly bowled off my feet by your lovely expression of congratulation. Scheduling now mildly disquieting – my garden best in later summer. How long will you be here? Letter follows.

Leslie

P.S. No, I'm not Lithuanian. My family on both sides came to the U.S. some time ago, from Russia and Hungary, mostly. Bill is half Lithuanian (the paternal half) but doesn't seem to feel connected to the current tragedy that way. Both of us just generally sorrowful as world citizens.

Clinton Corners, N.Y.

Dear Roger,

BILL: What could be better than the arrival of your new book, timed perfectly with the new crop of dark morels? Mushroom picking by day, eating by dusk, and reading in bed till the lights go out!

What a lovely addition to our library. As always the clean Phillips style illuminates many of those dark areas that even classic texts leave behind. 'So, that's what a Burgundy-Buff Cap looks like!' I am sure it will be one of those books used quite a bit, and for me a special thrill since I watched you photograph so many of them while at the several forays we worked together.

Congratulations, Roger. I hope you sell a million!!!

LESLIE: Me too, says Leslie, who has yet to give the *opus splendiferous* more than an envious glance. I could blame it on the ol' mega-workload, but the real problem is those morels! Paradise. B. of course knows all the spots and the one we've been visiting is extraordinarily appealing even without the mushrooms. An old estate grown over with woods and scrub, every now and again a huge specimen tree, clump of daffodils. B. found one cluster of black beauties rising through the carpet of yellow petals under a vast forsythia. No camera along, of course. I think I'll get one of those itty bitty numbers like spies have, small enough to shove in a back pocket.

BILL: Chapter Two: other events in our life. Perhaps Leslie has told you that we are about to buy a big old house. Old for the US of A means Civil War stuff. Big as in a ten-room colonial.

Leslie says it is still a bit small, what with this and what with that. An office here, an office there, here a greenhouse, there a laundry, and before you know it we will have to build an addition just to have adequate guest room. You had better come soon, before it all gets eaten up.

The summer will bring with it all the thrills of two homes and two gardens. Grand designs in both places, if you please. Spring is such a nice place from which to dream. Everything here is as tendergreen as it gets, no weeds, just gardens perfect in their plan, stretched out across the imagination of our yards. It is America, Roger. Dreams unconstrained by other nations, other people, creatures . . . As of yet insects do not appear to chew our lettuces, or molest our tomatoes or squash.

LESLIE: The frigging deer, however, have trimmed the ancient yews in the yard of the new house to the most fantastical shapes – hideous beyond imagining, probably irreparable and there you are. My dreams mostly involve chain saws and backhoes.

BILL: Leslie has been frantically packing essential items in boxes even as we write. She intends to hit the road tomorrow. Has been saying that for the past week. She's off to Maine and the gardens hewn out of the wilderness. I am led to believe it is all blackflies and mud there now. Better to send her off to get it all cleared. I'll stay behind and thoroughly enjoy this spring, then get along up north for the summer-spring of mid-coast Maine in July and August. See you then. Chanterelle time, I presume.

LESLIE: Let him gloat, I figure I'll finally have a little peace and quiet (pace the blackflies) to get some work done, and, if I plan it right, a second spring complete with lilacs and my many tulips. No one around here – at least no one visible from the roads – seems to be capable of anything except red and yellow Darwins. Handsome enough in their way but a bit boresome after a while. The same cannot be said of the dogwood, at its peak right now and indeed very hard to leave. B. helped clean up the garden last fall, so I'm hoping that getting it going again won't be too difficult, especially since in view of my changed circumstances I was very restrained in the perennial-ordering and annual starting departments. The whole problem of delegating basic garden functions turns out to be a very interesting one and how well I've solved it remains to be seen.

Enough! packing calls (at least it calls me, and I've decided it's not fair for him to have the last word – unless of course he wishes to say something blanket-affectionate, to match the assorted friendly sentiments I send myself . . .!)

BILL: It's a very nice book. One I have been waiting for a long time.
Thanks again . . . B

Cushing, Maine

May 15 1991

Dear Roger,

Here's what I think, now that I'm home:

Narcissus are very nice, the scent of hyacinth is such as dreams are made on, but it is in tulips lies the preservation of the world. I've decided it's humanly impossible to plant too many, assuming, of course, you're not using them to spell out your company logo in red and yellow or something like that. (Poor cannas, by the way, talk about a magnificent flower damned to ignominy by ill-use!)

I have both made and seen any number of effective tulip beds, but I still think they shine brightest indoors and have an old blue mason jar of them on the desk this very minute. A vase of flowers carries an implicit suggestion of order, a suggestion to which said desk has no right, being as it is in very nearly terminal disarray. But the tulips in their incongruity are saviours against madness. For one thing, they're huge – so immense they take up enough space to block out a fair amount of muddle. For another, they're pretty close to terminally disarrayed themselves. A parrot tulip in the last full blown stages is blowsiness personified. Yet even at the edge of decay the fleshy petals are still turgid, their color layered shimmering and satiny. These happen to be 'Estella Rijnvelds', red, pink and white, with brushes of green. 'Black Parrot' is worth the price of admission, too, and so is the dark red 'Wonder' I've mentioned before. The paler ones don't do so well; they tend to start turning brown sooner, before they really hit that moment of total relaxed exposure.

The other thing I love is the way tulips are their own arrangement, stems and blossoms slowly turning and bending, changing with each passing day. Greenery, other

135

flowers, all the arrangers' embellishments only confuse the issue. I'm not saying they don't enhance mixed bouquets – vaguely Dutch assortments of peonies, roses and tulips are practically a trademark of *luxe* decor and rightly so – but tulips never need accompaniment themselves and are always prettiest I think without bother or fussiness.

I concentrate on the cottages, Darwins, and super-late types like parrots and lilies, for a good solid six weeks of The Joy of Tulips. I know I could get more if I could bring myself to like species tulips, but I can't. Either, like *Kaufmannianas*, their proportions are all wrong: great big flowers on short stems and a general effect of consummate squattiness, or, like *T. sylvestris*, they are in proportion, hence delicate, hence much more like true wild flowers which are fine but not tulips.

They're about the only ones, on the other hand, that I enjoy seeing sprinkled here and there under the trees. Tulip beds are okay – I guess – in large public gardens and similar well-manicured venues, and a long-lived survivor in a weedy dooryard has undeniable nostalgic charm, but as far as I'm concerned tulips are too intentional to do well as part of the landscape. To me, they're a crop, more like strawberries than snowdrops, and I plant the bulk of them in the vegetable garden.

This has the benefit of forcing me each fall to think a bit about next year's garden, because I put the tulips where hills of winter squash will be planted. At this point it's mostly force of habit; I once thought the spreading vines would hide the ripening bulb foliage. Which they would in a warmer climate. Here spring is usually too cold for any such tidiness. By the time the squash gets lush, the tulips have already been looking tatty for ages. Still, it does keep them nicely out of the way, and the squash vines are over in plenty of time for me to dig up the bulbs, separate, and replant in fertilized ground. Where, of course, they will fail to bloom, having just split in half. It takes *years* for them to recover and I'm not entirely sure it's worth it. Limited income notwithstanding, I think from now on I'll just let 'em go and buy new each autumn as necessary.

It's like hilling up tea roses for winter, which at this point I seldom do. Wind and cold always decimate them at the very least, the hilling is a chore – you've got to get the soil from somewhere and then take it *to* somewhere; and since early planted new bushes usually do do splendidly all summer and fall, I've decided that in Maine tea roses should be treated as annuals.

Shrubs, of course, are a different matter. I feel about 'La Reine des Violettes' the way I do about sweet peas and old-fashioned tomatoes: come hell or high water, whatever it takes.

Time, mostly. I thought I could just come back and resume but of course the weeds are way out ahead and planting is way behind. So –

More soon,

Leslie

P.S. Suddenly had a horrified thought – *You* don't have tulip beds, do you? Somehow I see yours nicely scattered about amongst the shrubbery *but* . . . Anyway, no offence meant. If you have beds, I'll bet they look great.

The Marquette Hotel, Minneapolis

18 May 1991

Dear Leslie,

I am out in the Midwest promoting *Mushrooms*, a ten-city tour no less – a city a day; New York, Boston, Minneapolis, Los Angeles, San Francisco, Seattle, Portland, Denver, Chicago and then Bernardsville in New Jersey. Three days down and seven to go. Will I make it? God knows. So far I am having fun meeting 'mushroom maniacs' in every city, all with morel stories to tell. Yesterday I did a programme for local public radio here with Steve Benson called 'Talking Sense'. Also on were Lee Mugli and John Ratzloff, author of *A Guide for Rooms*, a whole book of morel mushroom jokes. Anyway, we all told terrible morel stories and had a big laugh – mushroomers are worse than fishermen for telling the tall story. I have made a morel flute – if you blow across *the stem* of a dried morel you get the Morel Hunters' call to arms.

The centre of Minneapolis is riddled with things called sky walks. One floor up from the ground you walk through these glass tunnels from building to building then right through the shops on that floor of the building and out across another street on another tunnel bridge. One of the locals told me that in the winter many people don't go out of doors for months. It all gave me a horrible shock of *déjà vu*. Here I was in Fritz Lang's Metropolis at last.

It seems about a thousand years since I wrote so let me go back a bit. We had a hard winter this year, the first one for four years – all those lovely tender plants I have been nursing along got hit. In fact I kept a record of what happened so that I will know what plants survive what temperature.

Exciting news. Three weeks ago a man called Philip Lloyd rang me up. 'Are you the chairman of The Society for the Protection of London Squares?' he asked. When I affirmed that I was he asked if he could come over, which he did right away.

It turned out that he worked for a Japanese property company called Fujita. Fujita had bought about half the houses in a little square in Bayswater just across Hyde Park from us. On looking into the deeds of the houses they discovered that they owned the square garden as well! After much chat, Philip asked me if I would do a survey of the current square, a plan of what the planting might have been one hundred and fifty years ago when it was built and a third plan of what I thought would be the way to relandscape and replant it to make it one of the best squares in London! Then he gave me about four days to do the lot. But actually this is the way I love to work. I got straight down to it – did the survey at 5.00 a.m. the next morning. The square at present is a dump; virtually no plants, five or six London plane trees and every- thing overgrown and silted up so that even discovering where the beds and path were was an exercise in industrial archaeology. I drew rough plans, consulted Bean on the dates that plants and shrubs had come into cultivation in Britain to see that the things I suggested were possible in 1850, and was able to get the survey and the spec. 1850 plan done in about thirty-six hours. I then got a trained landscape architect to draw them up for me whilst I continued working on ideas for the way I would like to see the garden look if the money was there to do it.

Philip Lloyd had mentioned that John Claudius Loudon had lived within a few hundred yards of the site, though the garden of his house was destroyed years ago. This started me going. I went over to Vincent Square where the Royal Horticultural Society have their library and heaped a table up with his books and those of his wife. Did you know he only had one arm so couldn't write? – all his books were dictated to his very young wife. After his death his wife continued his great work with the most exquisite illustrated books on bulbs, annuals, perennials (in two volumes) and, finally, conservatory plants. Though she did them in a different order, these are exactly the same volumes that Martyn and I are in the middle of doing right now, down to the detail that we too have had to split perennials into two volumes.

The chance was there so I took it. What I did was move the paths to make a larger area at both ends of the square (it is, of course, a rectangle) so that I could have room for memorial areas for both the Loudons. At the more shady southern end I plan to plant a shrub garden given over entirely to a selection of the shrubs that John Claudius talks about in his major work on shrubs, published in 1825; they will all be grown as single specimens with little stepping stone paths between them so that you can get amongst them and really see how they grow. At the other end of the square, the northern end that gets more light, I am proposing a Mrs Loudon Flower Garden as a memorial to her and her work, naturally choosing plants and varieties that she illustrates in her books. These two plantings will be mainly hidden from view as you approach to give that element of change as you come upon them. In the centre of the garden I want a small delicate fountain approached through two lateral tunnels of climbing roses. The stepping-stone path that runs down the lawn will have bulbs planted through it so that in early spring there will be a wild area. I will send you copies of all the plans later.

The reason for the rush was that Mr and Mrs Fujita were making a world-wide tour of all their companies and were due in London in a few days. The whole party, about eight or nine, arrived – complete with interpreter – to see Eccleston Square on the Saturday morning. Nicky and my two girls, Phoebe (now eight) and Amy (five) gave them coffee and chocolate Bath Oliver biscuits. They seemed to enjoy the visit, although I think having two children at what could have been a boring old business meeting was what made it. They went back afterwards to the office and saw the plans – all is approved to go ahead with the Loudon gardens.

The Japanese do everything in the most detailed and organized way and already I have had to submit a plan of what my involvement in the scheme would be plus a detailed bit of all the steps involved in laying out and planting a square – it runs to more than eighty steps.

The square, by the way, is called Craven Hill Gardens and was originally part of Lord Craven's estate. Before the houses were built it was designated as a plague pit. Luckily, although the land was held for this purpose for many years it was never used, even plagues go out of fashion.

On the Eccleston Square threat (now much reduced) I have written to the agents of the freeholders, presenting to them the idea that they might get some good publicity by giving the land to the Garden Committee. Reply: 'We are considering your proposal.' – Well anyway I tried.
Love,

Roger, and hugs to Bill.

Cushing, Maine

Dear Roger,

The reason you haven't heard is that I'm frantically trying to be sure you'll have something to *see* when you get here. Do not be away all spring and expect to walk in in mid May and plant, is my advice to you. Weeds? The word is inadequate. No question that for folks like me, gardening is a constant process of beating back the wilderness. Now I know why Lois, who doesn't get here until June, has always confined herself to a few perennials, a small vegetable patch and an occasional go at pruning.

Lois's vegetable garden is mostly grown over now – my place more than does for both of us – but her splendid rhubarb remains. It was on the property when she bought it thirty years ago and was already well established then. But part of making the place livable was completely rebuilding the plumbing system and when the man came with the backhoe he said, 'These giant rhubarb plants are right where I've got to dig for your septic tank. Would you like me to move them somewhere else, would you like to keep them?' She was newly up from the city and just sort of said 'Well yes, sure, of course I'd like to keep them. Put them over there,' and made a vague gesture in the direction of the barn. The fellow picked up these two enormous clumps of rhubarb with his backhoe and stuck them down near the barn where they have been ever since, thriving like crazy and very delicious. An uncommon kind, no-one knows what it is, not bright red at all but green with just a tiny tinge of red. In a good year the stalks will be two and a half feet long and completely tender from end to end and with a lovely flavor.

So, the rhubarb was at one end and then she had just a

conventional little vegetable garden, a rectangle where she had planted asparagus from seed, and lettuces and Swiss chard and carrots and beans and things like that, all of which would flourish until they were about two inches tall and then the woodchuck would come in and eat them, over and over and over again and Lois would go out and speak sternly to the woodchuck, which was quite tame, and we're talking years so it was like a family of woodchucks. I would come over to visit and there would be endless woodchuck stories because Lois had this Titanic struggle – or perhaps Sisyphean would be a better adjective. She tried mothballs, for instance, mothballs being an organic gardening device for keeping wood-chucks away, one of the many organic devices that don't work very well. So the woodchuck would go through the Maginot Line of mothballs and it went through criss-cross string and it went through bloodmeal and it went past the have-a-heart trap and on one memorable occasion she waited in the garden to whack it on the head with a stick and when she did it just kind of reared back and looked at *her* very sternly and she got scared and left.

The woodchucks continued to be an issue after I came and cleared and began making my garden. For several years I would go next door and borrow Edna's .22 and shoot them. It works in that the one you shoot stops eating but it's not completely satisfactory. Before long, others come to fill the void. Then one summer a family of skunks came to live under my house and the woodchucks disappeared. I don't know if it was the skunks, actually I think it may have been the raccoons, both the raccoons and skunks started coming at the same time. But when the two other creatures came the woodchucks went. I have no proof of cause and effect, and in fact they shouldn't occupy the same niche because they eat different things but whatever it was I'm glad it happened and I kind of enjoy the skunks.

They did a job, I'm sorry to say, on Lacey (Bill's

daughter's dog) when they were last here. Well the dog was barking so the skunks got defensive. They're very tame because they've been living comfortably under the summer house for years. I throw my meat scraps into the woods – there are lots of creatures there who like to eat stuff like chicken bones so what's the point in sending them to the landfill? I just fling out fish guts or fat I've trimmed off the steak ... whatever bits of carnivore garbage I have and basically what I'm doing is feeding the skunks. It's been live and let live. We've had a couple of meetings in the garden where everybody got a bit scared and backed off but I've never been afraid of them. Unfortunately last fall they got to eating the tulips. Bill when he was visiting had a couple of confrontations when he was standing close to the front door with this arsenal of rocks and throwing the rocks at the skunks and he actually hit them a couple of times and they would kind of amble off. You really would have had to kill one I think. So that was a kind of a stand off.

Apart from woodchuck prevention the thing they do which is quite wonderful is that they love to eat yellow jackets, wasps, any hive of those things gets torn apart. I think there must be sugar in the hives and I think maybe the insects themselves are tasty, insects are what skunks mostly eat, after all. Three weeks ago I was walking by the lower garden when I noticed the most tremendous nest of yellow jackets – they make the same kind of nest as wasps, a grey paper football – just merrily sitting there on the ground with yellow jackets coming and going quite close to the walkway. Then while I was dithering around and not having the time to go to town to the hardware store to buy some kind of ghastly yellow jacket poison, the skunks just came and ate them. Thus in my view skunks are sort of like bats, quite nice to look at, and so environmentally beneficial that I can't see any reason to evict them, besides which I don't know if I *could* evict them.

Regrettably they don't weed. I don't seem to do anything else. There is some revenge in the form of nearly-nightly dinners of lamb's quarters steam-fried in butter with garlic, but you can't get too excited about eating buttercups and witchgrass (poison and pure cellulose), my principal afflictions. What I do with those (and everything else in the vegetative waste department) is pile it at the southeast side of the upper garden where the ground slopes off precipitously. Under the pile are grocery sacks filled with newspapers, and the end result is (or is becoming) something approaching soil. I've been doing this for about three years, and in another year or two will no longer be in constant danger of falling backwards into the brambles when tending that side of the garden.

One year I piled hay bales there, building a sort of temporary raised terrace so I could plant a row of tall peas right at the edge of the world where they wouldn't be in the way. It was great for a while – I think the Great Wall of Hay kept the ground nicely cool and moist because the peas grew very tall and lush – but then most of the vines got gnawed off at about two inches above ground level because in piling up all those hay bales I had built the world's largest condominium for mice.

I use hay for mulch as well, and to cover the paths. It works very well as long as you keep after it, but it brings in so many weed seeds I'm thinking of switching to straw even though it is more expensive and less pleasant to walk barefoot on. A Pennsylvania woman named Ruth Stout once wrote a terrific book called *How to Have a Green Thumb Without an Aching Back* in which she advocated monster piles of straw mulch year round. She just kept piling it on, replenishing it as it broke down, and parted it, like the Red Sea, in order to plant. I don't remember what she did about the slugs. Pennsylvania is hot enough for year-round cool soil (if you left thick mulch on here that way you'd never see a tomato), and she kept the layer so thick the weeds were smothered before they got started.

Not an option in this semi-ornamental establishment, where the weeds have had the benefit not only of my absence but also of weather as warm as late July for most of May.

Dry as late July too. Everything, even the weeds, is just sitting there in the desert-like sand and trying not to die. Is this global warming? We are eating wild strawberries three weeks early, even as the last bits of lilac perfume the air. Bunchberry is still in flower, right next to the pink lady's slipper(!) Must say I've always wondered about that name. Could it be a corruption of something else the way foxglove is really folksglove? My friend Swy (Susan Wysocki) calls them scrotolota, which looks a lot more plausible. Or does slipper have other connotations and I'm just naive to think of shoes?

In the garden, all is fairly chaste unless you count a fair number of mating bugs. The hollyhocks haven't begun to bloom. I have again started some *clitoria* and am determined to find out this year if they really were named for their astonishing resemblance. (Dead ringers, except that they're a fine bright blue.) Common name for the wild form is 'butterfly pea', which doesn't sound especially promising. The seedlings are still in the greenhouse as I write, and mysteriously missing on top of that. The feminine form may be grossly underrepresented if they aren't found, because the sweet peas have been totally wiped out by the worst cutworms in years.

This is, in any case, not great sweet pea ground (too hot, sandy and acid) but I usually do okay, especially with the 'Floral Tribute' mixture from Thompson and Morgan. I had a fine stand of them coming up when I left for the last trip to N.Y., came home to find just a couple of sprouts, all the rest sawn off. Nothing for it but to replant with standard 'Spencers' from the farm store and hope for the best.

Weeds, cutworms, drought, the litany of my woes reminds me this is really more farm than garden in the growth as well as design departments. Being surrounded by fields doesn't help, and neither does having the annuals and perennials mixed in large beds where there is a lot of exposed soil all winter each year. Then I compound the problem by refusing to completely clean up in the fall (actually, not so much refusing as failing, what with this and what with that; but I do it at least partly to be rich in volunteers).

I am in total awe at your speed in researching and designing the Loudon gardens. What a marvellous commission! Let's hope the commissioners are as decisive as you are, since if things follow a normal course you will now get to hurry up and wait for months and months and months.

The plan certainly sounds delightful, a fine mix of aesthetics and education – be sure to keep me informed as the project goes forward. Will the folks whose houses border the square have any say, or does Fujita's ownership give them absolute control? I rather hope so, and not just for speed's sake. Surely after all your vicissitudes you'll agree that art by committee is oxymoronic, in the garden as much as or even more than anywhere else.

June 10

With the lilacs and tulips gone by, shirley poppies not yet started, the show is pretty thin right now unless you count the iris, which every year at this time I am reminded I should plant more of. And there is the hesperis. What a revelation. It's probably as common – and possibly as boring – to you as petunias and marigolds are here. But I had only read about it, never seen, or, more to the point, smelled it when I started the seeds last year. 'Dame's Rocket' sounded so enticing, so loaded with lovely cottage-garden associations that I went for it without stopping to think about where to put the plants. They languished in the trays for a while, ended up thrown in together in an out-of-the-way empty space and pretty much forgotten. Neglect didn't bother them, by midsummer they had made handsome green mounds about a foot tall. Then they almost got ripped out because the cabbage worms got to them; by the end of the season they were hideous testimony to the importance of BT (Bacillus thurigensisis, an organic pesticide that really *does* work, though you do have to keep at it).

But being me I didn't rip them out and this spring, well ahead of the wretched bugs, the four remaining plants have made a huge bush, almost five feet tall and that many around, covered with purple, pale violet and off-white flowers. The fragrance covers the whole garden at night, a mysterious mixture of lilac and clove.

Looking at a bunch of them on the kitchen table I'm struck by how much they do resemble lilacs, those innocent four-petalled, open flowers, yet everything about them is simpler, simultaneously coarser and more fragile. I'd say, 'Why on earth doesn't everybody grow them?' but I know the answer – they're biennials, gratification not only delayed but temporary.

Will close for now to get this in today's mail. Hope all's well, can't wait to see you.

Love,

Leslie

9 July 1991

Dear Leslie,

Before the other news let me thank you for your
wonderful book, it's got fun just leaping about all over the
pages. (*The Modern Country Cook* by Leslie Land, Viking
1991)

You went on and on about weeds, brambles, etc. in your
letter. Over the weekend I met a gardener who squatted a
lovely Victorian house in Brixton (South London). The garden grew only broken-down fridges, old cookers, rotting
carpet, broken glass, the whole grown over with a thick
layer of brambles. He, Marcus, has a solution, perma cul-
ture. Have you come across it? It's an Australian No Dig
system. All you do is slash down the weeds and brambles,
throw on a small amount of bonemeal and then cover the
whole thing with about twelve layers of wet newspaper. On
top you put a mulch of well-rotted stable manure about six
inches thick, you then plant your annuals or perennials
straight into it, the same day, giving them about three handfuls of soil each. If you want to plant shrubs you break a
small hole in the membrane and plant the shrub in the soil
and weeds below, then replace or renew the membrane right
up to the stem of the shrub. Water the whole thing well in
and bingo! a garden.

Do you remember I chatted on about sewing my annuals
on top of a deep layer of leaf mould? It has worked well and I
now have in flower about forty million opium poppies and
sweeps of our lovely wild larkspur, *Consolida ambigua*. Next
year I am going to put a dusting of blood, fish and bonemeal
on top before throwing on the seeds so that the leaf mould

will have a better balance of nutrients – but it works and it has kept the weeds right down.

I love dame's violet, sweet rocket, *Hesperis matronalis* or whatever you like to call it. I would love to get hold of a sack of seed, especially the white form. It would be wonderful in forests under the lilac where little grows because of the shade. But no seed merchant has it! Why not? Too common or wild I suppose. A sudden thought: maybe Suffolk Herbs have it? I checked in their wild flower seed catalogue and found it listed not as a wild flower but as a cottage garden flower! I am breaking off right now to send them a cheque for £12 to send me twenty packets.

I have got a most odd plant in the garden (I mentioned it before but this time I have done a sketch of the fruit), it was bought as the American woodland plant Doll's Eyes *Actaea pachypoda* but instead of one eye (berry) per stem it has a group of eyes – a composite eye like a fly. No book mentions it, what can it be?

My odd looking 'Doll's Eyes'

All over London this spring there have been problems with London plane trees, *Platanus acerifolia*. There is a fungus disease that attacks the leaves and leaf petioles and causes up to a 25 per cent leaf drop; there are also a great many dead trees, especially on the roadside, possibly killed by salting in the icy weather, or by the very dry summers we have had over the last few years. Possibly it is a combination of all three problems that is causing us to lose so many trees. Anyway I am nervous that in the future the problem may get worse. My only solution at the moment is that people should not plant so many planes: monoculture is at best of times a very dangerous thing, one only has to think of the Dutch elm disease to realize how devastating the results can be. Anyway my advice to people who have asked is: diversity.

When we had our really cold spell at the end of January I kept a record of what I thought might get damaged or killed by frost. Anyway read it through and you will see what winters in central London are really like.

Tender Plants Report February 1991

For four winters we have had virtually no frosts, a matter of down to 28F (−2C) at night rising above freezing during the day. This has gradually led to an increase in the number of more tender plants in the garden.

February 2–5 we had night-time lows of 27F (−2½C), with the temperature rising to about 34F (1C) during the day.
Feb 6 low 26F (−3C) high 31F (−½C), ½" of snow. The wind-chill factor is rather low at the moment; a very slight breeze from the east, perhaps 5 m.p.h.
Feb 7 low 22F (−5C) high 28F (−2C), 4" fall of snow.
Feb 8 low 22F (−5C) high 28F (−2C), 4" snow. Wind 5 m.p.h. north east.
Feb 9 low 18F (−8C), high 31F (−½C), 1" snow. Some sun.
Feb 10 low 24F (−4C), high 32F (0C). A little sun.
Feb 11 low 28F (−2C), high 37F (3C). A few hours of sun.

Feb 12 low 25F (−3½C), high 36F (2C).
Feb 13 low 29F (−1½C), high 37F (2½C).
Feb 14 low 25F (−3½C)), high 40F (4C), a few hours of sun, the wind very slight from the south west.
Feb 15 low 28F (−2C), high 44F (6C), there has been some light rain and the snow is thawing very rapidly.
Feb 16 low 28F (−2C), high 46F (7C).
Feb 17 low 31F (−½C), high 46F (7C).
Feb 18 low 32F (0C), high 44F (6C).
Feb 19 low 25F (−3½C), high 45F (6½C).
Feb 20 low 28F (−2C), high 44F (6C).

At this point I am stopping the records as the cold spell seems to be over. The temperature stayed well above freezing last night 40F (4C). When the cold weather started I was able to bring a few pots in from the garden to my back yard where the temperatures would be about 3F (1½C) above those in the garden but with no wind-chill factor to allow for. These pots were put back out in the garden on February 18.

LIST OF THE MAIN PLANTS IN THE GARDEN THAT ARE THOUGHT TO BE SUBJECT TO FROST DAMAGE

Abutilon ('Canary Bird') wire basket full of leaf-mould surrounds trunk up to 2′. I have pruned it back, as I would anyway have done and it is now showing signs of shooting away.

Acacia baileyana wire basket full of leaf-mould surrounds trunk up to 2′. As soon as the weather started to warm up it became apparent that the branches of the Mimosa had all got fine lateral cracks. By March 18 all the leaves have died and the branches have turned from their fresh grey-green colour to a dull brown, I am hanging on in the hope that it will start to break, but it seems doubtful. June 1 dead as the proverbial doornail. July 1, wrong again, thank goodness I hung on to it, I went out and told Arthur to dig it out when we saw that the good wood on the trunk that had been protected with the leaf-mould was just beginning to break!

Albizia julibrissin leaf-mould 1′ high round base, this year even the young shoots have not gone back at all, what seems to happen is that if you get a good hot summer especially with late season hot days the wood matures properly and will withstand any old temperature; however if the late summer is cold and damp the new wood will die back at the first sign of frost. No damage shows at all by March 18.

Alyogyne hakeifolia (Mediterranean) in my back yard, it went back out into the garden at the beginning of March and is fine.

Ballota acetabulosa, in pots on the patio, it has died right back and at March 18 shows no sign of recovery. April 30 pronounced dead and removed.

Bougainvillea in Bed 25, no protection. April 30 looks completely dead but I will give them another few weeks to see if they move at all. Later dead.

Bougainvillea in a large pot on the patio, leaf-mould 6″ high round base. Dead.

Bougainvillea in a pot in my back yard during the very cold spell. Dead.

Callistemon citrinus leaf-mould 6″ high round base, the leaves are a little damaged.

Callistemon pallidus leaf-mould 6″ high round base, the leaves and the tips of the young shoots are slightly damaged.

Camellia cultivars as per list unprotected, I can see no damage and by March 18 many are flowering well.

Camellia sasanqua unprotected, one specimen, 'Narumi-gata' is rather badly burnt, it is in rather an exposed situation, I shall move it to a more protected position.

Camellia cuspidator unprotected, fine.

Camellia saluenensis unprotected, fine.

Cantua buxifolia (Mediterranean) in my back yard, it went back out at the beginning of March and is doing well.

Ceanothus species and cultivars (38) as per list 1st-year plants with plastic bags over them and leaf-mould to about 6″ deep at base.

Ceanothus 'Burkwoodii' is the only one that is damaged, both of our specimens are rather badly burnt although only a few small branches have died back.

Choisya ternata unprotected. No damage.

Choisya 'Aztec Pearl' unprotected. No damage.

Cistus unprotected, no problems.

Clianthus puniceus leaf-mould 6″ high round base. The plant was covered in flower buds when the frost hit; about 75% of which have been killed, otherwise only the top 3–4 inches of the branches have died back. Quite a lot of flowers through May.

Coronilla valentina subsp. *glauca* (herb beds) unprotected, no problems.

Chrysanthemum frutescens (bush daisy), they look very badly damaged, all the leaves and young shoots are black. They are all dead. I have cuttings in the tunnel which have survived.

Crinodendron hookerianum unprotected, the leaves are a little burnt at the tips but the profuse flower buds are looking most healthy.

Crinodendron patagua unprotected, the leaves are a little burned.

Cytisus battandieri (Pineapple Plant) leaf-mould 6″ high round base. No damage.

Cytisus maderensis (Beryl's Bed), the leaves have all been burnt off but by March 18 it is showing new shoots all over.

Datura (*arborea* ?) wire basket full of leaf-mould surrounds trunk up to 2'. As the weather starts to warm up a little, some cracks can be seen in the old wood, the young shoots and leaves have all gone completely soft and are just hanging deadly down. Early March I cut it back to just the main stem, all the rest of the wood was already going rotten. March 18 right at the base it is showing signs of breaking. Coming back well June 5.

Ebenus cretica (Mediterranean) in my back yard, it went back out at the beginning of March and is doing well.

Echium fastuosum leaf-mould 6" high round base, some cracks are showing in the main stems as the weather warms up a little, all the leaves and flower buds are black and very dead. March 18, yes it is completely dead and now gone.

Echium pinaniana wire basket full of leaf-mould surrounds trunk up to 2'. The leaves were badly burned, but a week later it is impossible to judge if the growing tip is killed off or not. Three more weeks later and it is confirmed as completely dead.

Escallonia unprotected, undamaged.

Eucryphia 'Nymansay' unprotected, some of the leaves are burnt.

Feijoa sellowiana leaf-mould 6" high round base, undamaged.

Fremontodendron 'Californian Glory' wire basket full of leaf-mould surrounds trunk up to 2', no damage.

Fuchsia (large standards in pots) leaf-mould 6" high round base. March 18 no sign of life yet. April 30 the tall stems of the standards have been cut back right to the ground, from which new healthy shoots are now appearing.

Genista aetnensis unprotected, undamaged.

Geraniums (scented leaf) unprotected, they have suffered very badly, the stems are all badly frosted, I will not remove them completely in the hope that they will break from the roots. March 18 there seems to be no hope of them coming back, so out they must go. I have cuttings in my little tunnel which have survived.

Griselina littoralis unprotected, looks fine.

Grevillea rosmarinifolia unprotected, March 18 the leaves have died back, but they look as if they will come back OK.

Hebes unprotected, there is some damage on the large-leaved more tender ones.

Hibiscus unprotected, no problems.

Hoheria lyallii unprotected, March 18, a few young branches have died back a bit but otherwise they are beginning to shoot.

Lavatera olbia (the common one) unprotected. Only the very tips of the young growth were frosted. Coming back well.

Lavatera assurgentiflora 'Barnsley' unprotected. Only the very tips of the young growth were frosted. Coming back well.

Leptospermum lanigerum unprotected, no damage.

Leycesteria formosa (Himalyan Honeysuckle) unprotected, no damage.

Lupinus arboreus leaf-mould 6″ high round base, a few of the stems were broken by the snow but otherwise it seems OK, but it is amongst other shrubs and therefore well protected.

Magnolia grandiflora unprotected, no damage.

Nerium oleander (in pots on the patio) wire basket full of leaf-mould surrounds trunk up to 2′ (one), (two) leaf-mould 6″ deep at base. The main stems have died back to about one foot above ground but below that they are coming back well.

Olea europaea (Olive) leaf-mould 6″ high round base. Badly frosted above the protection, the bark is all split and starting to peel off after only a week or so. Despite this damage it all seems to be throwing new leaves; perhaps this sort of reaction to frost is what gives ancient olive trees their wonderful characterful gnarled appearance.

Osteospermum in beds unprotected. The stems have all been killed off by the frost, the question is will they come back from the roots. About half of the plants have been lost including 'Whirligig' which seems the most tender.

Osteospermum cuttings in tunnel. By March 12 they have made terrific roots and I have now potted them up.

Pelargoniums unprotected. Completely killed.

Pittosporum tenuifolium 'Purpureum' unprotected, undamaged.

Pittosporum tenuifolium 'Variegatum' unprotected, undamaged.

Pittosporum tobira unprotected, undamaged. This is a really good plant not planted enough in my opinion.

Senecio greyi, unprotected, undamaged. The cuttings that I put in my tunnel have all made terrific roots and are now (March 12) potted up.

Senecio rotundifolia (*Brachyglottis rotundifolia*) unprotected, just about 6 leaves have dropped off, otherwise no damage.

Tropaeolum tuberosum (tubers about 3″ down in the soil), March 18 a few of them are starting to come through now so obviously they have survived.

Wattakaka sinensis (Climber) unprotected. April 30 new growth breaking out.

Back to early flowering perennials. Have you ever tried woad? I love my great misty yellow mounds in late April or May – this is another thing I will plant more clumps of.

We leave for the States in six days so the next contact will be hugs on your step. So excited to see the garden – keep weeding – keep watering – keep deadheading – keep cooking – here we come.
Love,

Roger

Cushing, Maine

Roger,

We are having hurricane Bob. It's about 7.30 in the evening now and the edge if not the eye is upon us. We have had just buckets, sheets of rain like you can't believe and the winds are very high but I don't think, looking out of the window at everything madly tossing about, that they are anywhere near the hundred miles per hour that everybody on the radio has been talking about all afternoon.

So far damage is minimal. The lattice work tomato support in the center of the upper garden, the one that sits perpendicular to the winds from the west has gone over, although this time it's in the winds from the east. All of the stakes holding up the sugar snaps in the lower garden are leaning at an assortment of crazy angles, and interestingly enough, so far the only big damage is the apple tree that Bill sawed out the middle of so that we could see the shore. The left hand part of the 'V' has now bitten the dust, or more accurately bitten the tomatoes and the delphiniums and everything else that was underneath it, and that has cleared a path for the winds to come across the lower garden and do even more damage. All of the trellised cucumbers are, of course, plastered to the ground, and the very very tall pink hollyhock, the twelve-foot one, is now leaning over at about forty-five degrees.

It will be interesting to see the damage. I mean I think to a large extent the damage will be the bruising of leaves. Probably won't know until tomorrow; it'll be abated before long but it's also coming dark. There are a lot of leaves on the grass which will now of course be greener and greener and greener and so far I would say I'm getting more benefit than harm. Bill took the pump out of the pond, cheerfully remarking that I probably would not have any further need of it this year and I think he must surely be right.

So far the little peach tree which isn't in really good condition, which I fear may not make it through the storm, is holding up and the greenhouse is still in place. We had a lot of talk as to whether the greenhouse could survive and if the winds really were a hundred miles per hour I doubt that it could; but I opened the doors at both ends so that the wind could whistle through and that's what it seems to be doing and that's also to some extent what it seems to be doing to the teepees that hold up those hyacinth (*Dolichos lablab*) beans and the teepee that holds up the currant tomatoes.

The central path is impassable, all of the artemisia has gone over and I think I will walk around until I can take a picture of it because it's making a very beautiful shape. You remember that the white phlox, which is now blooming in earnest, had already begun to close that opening under the archway and make a pretty shape against the path? Now there is a folded quality, an almost woven quality, with the bright green phloxes rising behind the grey-green of the artemisia. The alyssum is in full carpet and it leads up in a kind of cream white and then the white is sort of cleansed as it hits the phlox's tops. The thyme is still blooming but the bloom is near the end so there's a greyness under the purple that picks up the grey of the artemisia. Not so pleasing is the sight of the beautiful blooming acidanthera in the window boxes at perilous angles; but so far that shape with all of the white morning glories and the asarina climbing the strings has not broken. All I did was staple the strings to the frame of the house but at this point in mid-storm they are okay. It'll be interesting to see what happens when the wind backs around and comes from the west because that's where it can get a good run-up across the open spread of field. I'm pretty protected from the east by all of that scrub and second growth. So far only old age and the prudence that comes therewith is keeping me from taking a walk because it's beautiful and it's very warm (almost tropical). So far we still have power. The lights flickered a couple of times but on the news on the radio they were saying that one hundred thousand households in Massachusets have lost power and on and on in the usual litany of hurricane woes so I may be speaking prematurely.

It's now August 27. It's hot, muggy, might as well be the dog days, just thick and wretched and miserable but the garden did in fact weather the storm very well. The entire garden has come a long way since you were here. All of the things that were naked and tiny and not pretty then, encouraged by the rain of the hurricane and just by the passage of time, are now larger and blooming. The central white path, although nothing like its usual self, has the handsomeness that I look forward to each year. The phlox is bloom-city. It's a little shorter than usual, which means it's about three feet tall, but very floriferous and not a trace of mildew. The cosmos has started to bloom in earnest. A lot of it did go over in the storm and I let it lie so that instead of these feathery green bushes with beautiful flat candid flowers, what I have is an intermingling of the foliage with the foliage of the alyssum and the portulaca and these flat white flowers looking up at you from various recumbent positions and that turns out to be very effective.

In addition to all this, there is *piccolino* basil (Bush Basil, *Ocimum minimum*) in the alyssum. I've a friend who calls it Afro-basil because it looks like it's been given one of those bushy haircuts. It has tiny very pungent leaves and right now each bush is maybe about a foot and a half across and the same height, a very tidy little mound. They are just about to bloom, so what you have is the standard main leaves of the bush which are dark green and about a half inch long, then the flowering stems which are a pale chartreuse, with leaves about a quarter or an eighth of an inch long, and presently it will be making white flowers.

TORONJIL
Red stems and
leaf edges

strong lemon scent

Next year, I think I'll put some *toronjil* (*dalea* species) in that section. Do you remember the *toronjil*, the Mexican marvel that grows right next to the Joe Pye weed, the thing that looks like mimosa but isn't? It closes at night but doesn't close at the touch. Tiny bluish leaves with a beautiful delicate red edge, and good sized, eventually gets to about four feet though this year I don't think it will on account of the drought. I got it to flower last year for the first time because I potted one and put it in the greenhouse. It made extremely petite flowers which I remember, probably inaccurately, as a kind of purply pink but it did not make seeds. I'm sorry I forgot to put it in anything I cooked while you were here. It has a unique, delicious, lemon/pepper/camphor scent, but only when very fresh. The perfume dissipates within hours and the dried herb is dust. Perhaps that's why it isn't better known. Seed, purportedly collected by Zapotecs in southern Oaxaca, Mexico, is from J. L. Hudson, P.O. Box 1052, Redwood City, Cal. 94604.

The Gaura (*Gaura lindheimeri*) is just beginning, barely, to bloom and its – honesty compels me to say – rather weedy-looking arching arms are reaching out. They do go well with all of those low matty things, though, because they put in a little bit of height. All of the white bee balm (*Monarda didyma*

'Snow Maiden') is blooming. The white is not strong, it's not like the white of the lavatera next to it (*Lavatera* 'Mont Blanc'), which is a very pure, intense, laundry-line white sheet white that just shines from the bushes. The monarda continues to be dark green on the old growth and chartreuse on the new growth and brown and silver where the painted lady butterflies are all over it. They really are having a good time whereas the bees appear uninterested.

The datura which was so paltry a month ago is now beginning to bloom. It's the nameless one from my neighbor. Very low and bushy, not one of those big majestic items and I'm sorry to say it's not particularly fragrant so I guess it isn't *metaloides*, though the leaves are very blue. Enormous great white trumpety flowers, though, big even for datura, that are perhaps most striking before they open. You get a long calyx, maybe four or five inches, out of which the flower rises and the flower is very long too, a cream color before it opens to white. It's a perfect closed whirl with five sharp points and then very very slowly they unfold and unwind themselves.

The *Nicotiana sylvestris* is also starting; at this point what I mostly have is fragrance and suggestion but the big flat leaves promise monstrous plants; as far as I can tell it will probably be just at its apotheosis when I leave for New York. The poison (I knuckled under and put some on the roses) seems effective. They're covered with buds but I don't yet know if the thrips have been conquered.

In the center beds a lot has come along, in particular the gladioli, which I think were not even in bud at the beginning of August. The ones in the front bed are not only blooming but probably at their height right now and all four beds are filled. I have a total of probably forty or fifty bulbs of a variety called 'Zigeunerbaron'; it's a quite remarkable plum color with strange pink shadings down the middle, and as it ages it goes to a dark, silvery lilac. It's about the color of a bruise, quite unlike any gladiolus you normally see, and it's particularly effective with the very dark maroon Centaureas (*C. cyanus*, seedling variety) and all of the assorted annual asters which are intense candy pink and a beautiful true violet as well as strong purple. All of that is backed at the western edge of the garden by the hot (color) bed with all of the screaming yellows and oranges: calendulas, tithonias, montbretias, etc., and the last of the yellow asiatic lilies which you see distantly behind this pink and purple event in the front.

It's stunning, though you do have to view it through the weeds because at this point I am no longer really trying to maintain the garden for this year but to cut back and prune and mulch and organize and start to get ready to go away to live with Bill. I'm very much looking at the garden now with the eyes of someone who is going to change it substantially, smarten it up and make it more suitable for being here only two months of the year; but still I don't know what all is going to be entailed there.

Leslie

P.S. I have to tell you your always enthralling diagrams and lists are also intimidating. There's nothing comparable here, but I'm enclosing a guide to the white garden, just to give an idea. Your midsummer visit made me acutely aware of a gap – the peaks of gorgeousness in this garden are definitely spring, *early* summer and fall. Now that I'm going to be a midsummer visitor myself – well, that's exaggerated, but you know what I mean – I'll have to concentrate on altering what have become very familiar rhythms.

WHITE GARDEN

1. *Arrhenatherum elatius (bulbosum)*
2. *Thymus praecox* subsp. *articus*
3. *T. pseudolanuginosus*
4. *T. citriodorus*
5. *Dianthus arenarius*
6. *Allium tuberosum*
7. *Satureja montana*
8. *Dahlia* × *cultorum* 'White Spider'
9. *Ocimum basilicum* 'Minimum'
10. *Silene maritima* 'Robin White Breast'
11. *Gladiolus hortanus* 'White Friendship'
12. *Gypsophila paniculata*
13. *Portulaca grandiflora* 'Swanlake'
14. *Salvia argentea*
15. *Artemisia dranunculus* var. *sativa*
16. *Levisticum officinale*
17. *Thuja occidentalis* 'douglasii pyramidalis'
18. *Rosa rugosa* 'Blanc Double de Coubert'
19. *Salvia officialis*
20. *Allium schoenoprasum*
21. *Dahlia* × *cultorum* 'Waterlily' (white selection from mixture)
22. *Phlox carolina* 'Miss Lingard'
23. *Iris sibirica* unnamed gift, small white flowers with bit of yellow
24. *Phlox decussata (paniculata)* 'White Admiral'
25. *Eschscholzia californicum* 'Milky White'
26. *Petroselinum crispum* 'Giant Italian'
27. Hybrid Tea Rose 'White Lightnin''
28. Climbing rose 'New Dawn'
29. *Clematis maximowicziana (C. paniculata)*
30. *Artemesia ludoviciana* var. *albula* 'Silver King'
31. *Nicotiana sylvestris*
32. *Lilium candidum (L. regale)* 'Black Dragon'
33. *Angelica archangelica*
34. *Lobularia maritima* 'Carpet of Snow' and 'Snow Crystals'
35. *Echinacea purpurea* 'White Swan'
36. *Monarda didyma* 'Snow Maiden'
37. *Scabiosa caucasica* 'Miss Willmott'
38. *Heracleum villosum*
39. *Diantus chinensis (heddewigii)* 'Black and White Minstrels'
40. Floribunda Rose 'Iceberg'
41. *Achillea ptarmica* 'The Pearl'

Detail of under garden and border, Upper garden, looking [...]

42. White peony 'Elsa Sass'
43. *Hydrangea paniculata* 'grandiflora'
44. *Lavatera trimestris* 'Mont Blanc'
45. *Dicentra spectabilis* var. *alba* followed by Oriental hybrid lily 'Casa Blanca'
46. *Delphinium elatum* 'Galahad'
47. *Cimicifuga racemosa*
48. *Crambe cordifolia*
49. *Digitalis purpurea* 'Alba'
50. White peony 'Florence Nicholls'
51. Ground Cover Rose (company definition) 'Alba Meidiland' (TM)
52. Antique Shrub rose 'Duchesse de something or other' that I cannot find for the life of me
53. *Macleaya cordata*
54. *Anemone japonica* (*A.* × *hybrida*) 'Honorine Jobert'
55. *Lychnis coronaria* 'Alba'
56. Climbing Rose 'White Dawn'
57. *Yucca filamentosa*
58. *Chrysanthemum parthenium*
59. *Cleome spinosa* 'Helen Campbell'
60. *Cosmos bipinnatus* 'Purity'
61. *Verbascum* – wild, probably *thapsus*
62. *Papaver somniferum* 'White Cloud'
63. *Gaura lindheimeri*
64. *Matthiola bicornis*
65. *Syringa vulgaris* 'Miss Ellen Willmott'

P/W This border does double duty, starting out in spring as a wash of shirley poppies, followed after the poppies finish (in early August) by cosmos, gaura, alyssum, and matthiola transplanted from across the path. Self-sown *Nicotiana affinis* is also allowed to grow here.

RB: Raised beds devoted to cutting flowers and vegetables

HB: Hot color beds

T: Teepee for growing bean vines or climbing tomatoes such as currant types

H: is the giant hackamatack, *Larix laricina*

14 October 1991

Leslie,

I really am a lazy old bugger, I've never ever written to
thank you for looking after us in the summer; it was really
terrific, especially getting a pair of Maine lobsters each! Also
whilst I am getting duties off my chest, thanks for the vegetable photographs; they were a very welcome addition to the
Vegetables book, which now only lacks black carrots and
some *Uluco*, another of those South American tubers. Martyn
goes to Mexico tomorrow – he may get them – or I may get
them in New Zealand in December when I go. Some of your
potato pictures are in Frankfurt at the Book Fair at this very
moment printed up for dummy spreads to sell the book to
overseas publishers. They look wonderful.

18 October

Finally the mushroom season has got going over here –
very late this year; normally the best time is the end of
September and the first week of October. Interest in fungal
things is growing apace. On Tuesday I did a radio broadcast
from Burnham Beeches relating fungus to the whole wood
ecology. On Wednesday I went with the TV South cook
from Sussex looking for mushrooms – he of course was only
interested in the edibles. On Saturday I am off to the New
Forest to take a group out on a general foray helping them to
identify and learn about all that we can find. Doing this much
in one week has helped me to define my position. I am an

White
cosmos

Monarda 'Alba'

Echinacea
'White Swan'

Shirley
poppies

Maine in August

amateur and all my books and my work are aimed at me. In other words, I go out and learn about a subject and then try and present it in a book, without patronizing other amateurs like me, who are in search of knowledge. In a sense I suppose I am a sort of bridge of communication between the academics with their complex language and ideas, and the keen but not academic naturalist or gardener.

As soon as I said that something was bound to give me my comeuppance. We have just been told we cannot put our garden waste in the giant bins that our local council have put on each corner of the garden. Years ago we used to burn our rubbish, especially the fallen leaves, but like good little citizens we have been trying to get greener and greener – indeed the council wrote to us and said that we must not burn! The vast majority of the leaves we chop up and compost down but of course there are many things like old stumps and roots that it is impossible for us to deal with. I suppose I will now have to take the whole matter up with the council and try to get a city decision on it – it's all mad, the street sweeper puts all his leaves in the big bins anyway.

This reminds me of another problem I had one summer. One of the more select ladies who live round the square rang me up and said, 'A young man and a young woman are making love in the bushes opposite my house, isn't it dreadful, the children might see or anything!' I said I would see what I could do about it. Fifteen minutes later (I judged this to be time enough even for the best of us) I went out to have a look, and duly found the young couple sitting quite respectfully on one of the benches smoking their post-coital cigarettes – leaving me with only one choice: say nothing. Is gardening a sex substitute? For the Greeks it was all about Zeus casting his seed upon mother earth. Perhaps it is simply that working close to the earth, with its fertility and the ever-present life and death of the seasons, gives you a more natural attitude to procreation as a fundamental fact.

Since seeing your garden in August I have been pondering the reasons for the difference of approach between our (English) and your (American) garden. My conclusions are not exactly momentous but here goes. English gardens always have straight edges, that is, they are formed within a rectangle or possibly a triangle; this affects the shape of everything; even if the gardener fights the geometry by having, say, two round lawns, there will still have to be beds around the lawns which back up to the rectangular edge. This shaping of the garden comes from the ancient use of the land and the way it is divided up into lots. Even when someone like a farmer builds a garden in the middle of a large area, they first divide it up into squares or rectangles. You only have to think about the way the grand houses had their lovely walled gardens to see the proof of that.

Your gardens, on the other hand, are often hacked out of woodland and have the appearance of a woodland clearing, and as the gardener gets more energy or has more time he hacks out another area of wilderness and turns it into a garden. The result is a shape that is never bounded by straight lines. So your yard/garden ranges from cultivated flowers to vegetables to wild flowers to totally wild woodland. It makes for a completely different feel from our rather geometrically formal approach.

This year snails have overtaken us. Next year I plan a concerted attack. One: discover where they overwinter and tread on them (they hide on flat, hard, hidden surfaces essential for them to stick to whilst they form the lid that covers the shell opening). Two: in the spring put down aluminium sulphate powder (it kills them off at a touch by stopping them making the mucilaginous slime essential to their movement; it does no harm to animals or birds, and has the added advantage of acidifying the soil – very good for camellias and hydrangeas, especially if you want blue flowers on the latter).

20 October 1991

Drunks in the garden again last night, one whisky bottle, one gin bottle, one vermouth bottle and many beer cans. They moved benches into the greenhouse – to sleep? – but did no damage apart from throwing-up on the path.
Love to you both,

Roger

Pleasant Valley, New York

Dear Roger,

The quinces are in the applesauce, the pumpkins carved, huge windrows of leaves – Bill rakes more daily – are piled in the new garden. Took the train to the city last week and got a second dose of leaf-peeping (got the first driving to Maine three weeks ago, rolling on for hours and hours through the oblivious autumn gorgeousness while on the radio the Judge Thomas hearings sleazed their way into history).

Last week was perfect, the sky forget-me-not blue, the Hudson the same, with a slate overlay. Between the tracks and the river a frieze of scrub flashed by, nothing but a blurred wash of bright yellow, bronze, green and brown with the occasional spark of magenta or crimson. Across the river, the hills were tapestried with second-flush colors: burgundy and brown-gold, ashes-of-rust ... *is* there such a color? I remember my mother being very fond of something called 'ashes of roses', pink with a silvery tinge to it, and this was the same, but dark orange.

And why tapestry? Why is that the autumn color cliché? Why don't we say 'It's like Seurat!', or 'Gee, Impressionism come to life', or something along those lines? At the height, heaven knows, it's bright enough, yet even the sumptuous reds of sumac and swamp maples don't remind us of paint. It must be that when we think 'tapestry' we are in the museum looking at old cloth, its vegetable dyes deep in the wool, shining out of the silk, part of the natural fabric. Of course, this may be on my mind because I just *saw* some gorgeous tapestries – in a show called 'circa 1492' at the National Gallery in Washington. I was down to take part in a seminar: 'Good as Gold, Foods the Americas Gave the World'. The usual litany, more or less: potatoes, corn, squash, beans, tomatoes, chocolate, peppers, a nod or two to amaranth, quinoa, manioc. (I'm attaching the list sent to participants.) It's really remarkable how airily we say 'the Americas' when so much came from Central and South America, so little from the North. (Wild rice, maple syrup, pecans and hickories, assorted helianthus . . .)

It's also remarkable how unwilling some people are to admit that scientists may not be able to fix everything. This was a pretty sedate gathering, not much in the way of Columbus-bashing or railing at the gastronomic, nutritional and social evils wrought by factory farming, but when we got to the preservation of genetic diversity . . . Well!

After a bit of public hot-and-heavy, I spoke with one of the science camp, trying to get him to admit that gene banks and academic grow-out projects, even if they were much more extensive and better funded than they are now, could never save all the species that currently exist, never mind duplicate the wide range of random conditions that ensure continuing mutation. His response was 'Oh, well, you're probably thinking of it as a gardener . . .' *Just* a gardener was richly implied in his patronizing tone. This led me to reflect on the contribution 'just gardeners' have always made and, by extension, the precarious position of amateurs in our time. I wanted to shake my fist in his face and say Gregor Mendel was an amateur and so was Thomas Jefferson and so are the farmers and gardeners who are right now growing, saving, and passing on thousands of cultivated varieties that would otherwise be lost.

Our 'heirloom seed' movement is still in its infancy, but it's growing all the time. No official support, of course, but private funding organizations are starting to take notice; both Kent Whealy, who started the Seed Savers Exchange, and Gary Nabham, of Native Seeds/Search, have won 'genius' grants from the MacArthur Foundation and the recognition those grants bring will probably be as important as the money. On the other hand, I'm afraid recognition is a mixed and not entirely durable blessing. I've dealt with several editors who said of old-fashioned seed-saving, 'We've done that story,' as though there were only one. The last piece I wrote about genetic preservation and the contribution of amateurs thereto was mercilessly dumbed down (readers were deemed incapable of understanding anything about the difference between 'hybrid' and 'open pollinated' except that a difference exists). And slick merchandizers are already jumping on the bandwagon now that 'Green' is hot in the marketplace. So I guess it won't be long before the pros take over.

Maybe it's romantic of me, and maybe I'm inspired by your happy example, but I have the sense that amateurs are better respected in Britain, that people there still see the Sunday painter and gentleman scholar as both admirable and capable. Here, on the other hand, we are obsessed with certified expertise. It's unlikely, for instance, that you'd have gotten to design the Loudon square unless you had a degree (or two) in landscape architecture. No matter how many societies you founded, how splendid your own gardens, how many books – actually, I take that back; the books would probably legitimize you. In the U.S., to write a book is to *be* an expert, Q.E.D., even if all you do in the book is prove that you don't know damn-all about the subject in question.

Cranky thoughts, and yet a minute ago I was thinking about how much I love forays, where intellectual democracy appears to be alive and well. The world of mycology seems unusually welcoming of dedicated amateurs, open-mindedly ready to accept people who don't have formal training. At the Rindge Foray, my first, I was amazed to see multi-degreed professors mingling with, actually paying attention to, the whole complement of amateurs. Everybody from experts like Bill, who's been at it for years, to the rankest beginner regarded as capable of valuable contributions.

Of course, at forays every pair of eyes and hands does help. When you've got three hundred people combing the territory nothing but mushrooms on their minds, even somebody who doesn't know a *gomphidius* from a *gomphus* may trip over something interesting purely by accident. But there's more to it than forays. Look at Bill's pal Peter Katsaros, an internationally known authority (admittedly, on slime molds) who has no academic credentials in the field at all. Maybe mycology is still comparatively open because there's so much that remains unknown about fungi, because so many fungi are themselves as yet 'undiscovered'. And maybe, come to think of it, it's because there's very little money to be made. I once asked Dick Homola (from the university of Maine, Orono), the only mycology professor I know, how many professional mycologists there are in this country. He allowed as how there were probably no more than a hundred or so, even counting the ones (it's the majority, I believe) who work for various industries. But all the same it never ceases to amaze me how many of the big names are people like Rod Tulloss. I mean, the guy is an engineer for the telephone company, yet he's also Mr Amanita, the fellow to whom everyone turns when there is a question about the genus.

And, of course, there is Roger Phillips Le Phillips himself!

But I digress. One thing that seems quite distinctively American to me is our use in gardens of unorthodox outbuildings and dependencies. For example we have not only Lo's big, serious barn and my not-so-serious plastic quonset hut greenhouse, we also have a storage shed (mine) and a chicken-house converted to a potting shed (hers); also an old outhouse, converted to a toolshed, a new outhouse (the one you call the compost loo), and an outdoor shower all of them

The Outhouse
-beshingled-

at Lo's. There's a root cellar, too, come to think of it, since the floor in the rock-walled basement of the old farmhouse is dirt. I use it to store dahlia bulbs, potatoes, beets, carrots, and bulbs for forcing, as well as wine and cheese.

Creative re-use of the buildings and the building of the loo are all Lo's doing. She has been getting maximum mileage out of everything for decades, was partial to simple solutions long years before such tendencies became politically correct. The old New England adage: 'Use it up, wear it out, make it do or do without', was just about invented to describe her, yet hers is not by any means a conventional frugality. I really think she finds waste aesthetically displeasing and is attracted to low-tech solutions because their simplicity is elegant in the long run.

The loo is a case in point, built after some years' consideration to take pressure off the bathroom, which is heavily used in high summer when we have a lot of visitors. Its resemblance to a tower folly (it has absolutely the best view of the upper garden anywhere on the property) is somewhat accidental, not so much a reaching for grandeur as a taking advantage of the way the barn is set. As you probably remember, entrance to the throne room is through Lois's studio on the main floor. Since we didn't go into mechanics when you were here, I'll explain that each of the two seats is at the top of a sealed, vented chute that leads to a holding tank (fifty-gallon oil drum) a full story below. The drums are mounted on jacks that are supposed to make it easy for Lo and me to move them without help; in practice the full ones are so heavy we usually get aid. But having to ask for additional muscle is the only obnoxious part. As long as each user is careful to 'flush' with enough peat moss to absorb all free liquid, the place doesn't smell, and each drum sits for about nine months before being emptied. By the time we turn out the contents the stuff is practically soil, but we give it a second composting, layered with garden waste and earth, just to be on the safe side.

Then, being very conservative types, we forbear to use it on the annual vegetables. We do use it on everything else: fruit trees, berries, and all the ornamentals. 'I'll give it a shot of our special mixture' is Lois's standard solution to any and all plant problems.

I think one reason it works so well is that we try not to pee in it any more than necessary. There's an old coffee can for urine, so we can use that at once before the nutrients leech away. Since urine is non-toxic when first expelled, all you have to do is dilute it with water so it doesn't burn the plants. Theoretically you could pour it right around the spinach, but what we mostly do is use it to spruce up the lawn: it greens up anaemic spots like some kind of miracle drug.

I don't need to tell you we've run into our share of sceptics, but not many the year of Lo's grand design. 1987, I think it was. She started just out of curiosity dumping her regular morning whizz in a straight line across the lower yard. Then she made a huge cross, then a many-rayed star, bright emerald against the grass green and clearly visible to even the most dull-sighted. Big success, though I don't think we actually *converted* anybody.

I'll close here for now, but there's *lots* more to come soon. Papa comes to visit tomorrow and I have to do everything right now but . . .

Love,

Leslie

Foods Originating in the Americas
(North, Central, and South America and the Caribbean)

CACTI:

Cactus pear (prickly pear) – *Opuntia spp.*
Nopales (cactus pads) – *Opuntia spp.*

FRUITS:

Atemoya – *Annona* hybrid
Avocado (alligator pear) – *Persea spp.*
Berries: Blueberries, highbush – *Vaccinium corymbosum*
                lowbush – *Vaccinium augustifolium*
       Cranberry – *Vaccinium macrocarpum*
       Huckleberry – *Gaylussacia baccata*
       Juneberry (service berry) – *Amelanchier spp.*
       Raspberry, American varieties (red) – *Rubus strigosus*
                    (black) – *Rubus occidentalis*

Strawberry – *Fragaria* hybrid (*F. virginiana*) and *F. chiloensis*
Cassabanana – *Sicana odorifera*
Ceriman (monstera) – *Monstera deliciosa*
Cherimoya – *Annona cherimola*
Cherries: Chokecherry (American wild cherry) – *Prunus virginiana*
Pin cherry (wild red cherry) – *Prunus pennsylvanica*
Rum cherry (sweet black cherry) – *Prunus serotina*
Custard apple – *Annona reticulata*
Feijoa (pineapple guava) – *Feijoa sellowiana*
Grape, scuppernong – *Vitis rotundifolia*
Granadillas: giant – *Passiflora ligularis*
sweet – *Passiflora quadrangularis*
Guanabana (soursop) – *Annona muricata*
Guava – *Psidium guajava*
Mamey – *Mammea americana*
Mamey sapote – *Pouteria sapota*
Naranjilla – *Solanum quitoense*
Papaya – *Carica papaya*
Passion fruit – *Passiflora edulis*
Pawpaw – *Asimina triloba*
Pepino (melon pear) – *Solanum muricatum*
Persimmon, American – *Diospyros virginiana*
Pineapple – *Ananas comosus*
Plums: American – *Prunus americana*
beach – *Prunus maritima*
Sapodilla – *Achras sapota*
Sugar apple (sweetsop) – *Annona squamosa*
Tamarillo (tree tomato) – *Cyphomandra betacea*
White sapote – *Casimiroa edulis*

GRAINS AND GRASSES:

Amaranth – *Amaranthus*
Corn, popcorn (maize) – *Zea mays*
Quinoa – *Chenopodium quinoa*
Wild rice – *Zizania aquatica*

LEGUMES:

Beans: Snap, string, green, yellow wax, navy, kidney, etc. – *Phaseolus
vulgaris*
Lima (butter) – *Phaseolus limensis*
Scarlet runner – *Phaseolus coccineus*
Tepary (Texas) – *Phaseolus acutifolius*
Peanut – Arachis hypogea

NUTS:

Black walnut – *Juglans nigra*
Brazil nut – *Bertholletia excelsa*
Butternut – *Juglans cinerea*
Cashew – *Anacardium occidentale*
Hickory nut – *Carya spp.*
Pecan – *Carya illinoensis*

POULTRY:

Turkey – Meleagris gallopavo

ROOTS AND TUBERS:

Arrowroot – *Maranta arundinacea*
Groundnut – *apios americana*
Jerusalem artichoke (sunchoke) – *Helianthus tuberosus*
Jicama – *Pachyrhizus erosus*
Malanga (yautia) – *Xanthosoma spp.*
Oca – *Oxalis crenata*
Potato – *Solanum tuberosum*
Sweet potatoes: North American – *Ipomoea batatas*
                          Boniato – *Ipomoea batatas*
Yuca (tapioca, cassava, manioc) – *Manihot esculenta*

SEEDS:

Pumpkin seeds – *Cururbita pepo*
Sunflower seeds – *Helianthus spp.*

SPICES, FLAVOURINGS, EXTRACTS:

Allspice – *Pimenta officinalis*
Capsicums (chili peppers) – *Capsicum annuum* and *Capsicum frutescens*
Cayenne – *Capsicum annuum*
Paprika – *Capsicum tetragonum*
Cassareep, basis of Worcestershire sauce, extracted from Yucca –
    Manihot esculenta
Chocolate, cocoa – *Theobroma cacao*
Maple syrup, sugar – *Acer saccharum*
Sarsaparilla extract – *Smilax spp.*
Sassafras extract – *Sassafras varifolium*

Spicebush berry – *Lindera benzoin*
Vanilla – *Vanilla planifolia*

VEGETABLES:

Capsicums (sweet and bell peppers, pimento) – *Capsicum annuum*
Chayote – *Sechium edule*
Gherkin (Jamaica cucumber) – *Cucumis anguria*
Pokeweed – *Phytolacca americana*
Pumpkins – *Cucurbita pepo*
Ramp (wild leek) – *Allium tricoccum*
Squashes: Winter (Hubbard, buttercup, crookneck, butternut,
                kabocha, etc.) – *Curcurbita maxima*
            Summer (yellow crookneck, zucchini, spaghetti squash, etc.)
                – *Cucurbita pepo*
            Calabaza – *Cucurbita moschata*
Tomatillo – *Physalis ixocarpa*
Tomato – *Lycopersicon esculentum*

FOOD-RELATED SUBSTANCES:

Annattio (food dye) – *Bixa orellana*
Beers made from corn, potatoes
Chicle latex (chewing gum) from sapodilla tree
Pulque (fermented maguey) – *Agave salmiana*
Quinine for tonic water – *Cinchona officinalis*
Tequila, distilled from pulque – *Agave tequilana*
Wines made from fruits

ECCLESTON SQUARE,
LONDON

18 November 1991

Leslie,

American autumn colour features in so many ads that we over here think it goes on all year over there. Our leaf change is minor compared with yours, yellows from the sycamores and browns from the oaks – reds are virtually nonexistent except for the occasional import – nevertheless they are much enjoyed.

Harking back to your loo (I suppose it may seem an excessive interest), a week or so ago there was an article about Abby Rockefeller, followed by a TV programme about her non-flush lavatory. She wants to potty train the world. Her system is much like yours except more expensive, more sophisticated and more mechanized. She allows two years to compost down but then she does use the result to grow what look like superb vegetables. The TV programme highlighted the dispute that the compost was not clean of the possible virus and bacterial infections that it could carry. It seems the State of California did tests to see what the virus situation was. The trouble was that they didn't actually test for the harmful viruses but some other kind of testing which came up negative, and they advised against the lavatories. Now I gather new tests have been done specifically looking for harmful virus and bacterial contamination and the results prove that the compost rates just the same as normal soil. Typical of the powers that be attempting to refute development with false information – will they never listen? Perhaps you, Lo and Abby should all get together and pool resources (information that is). I thought we were eating tomatoes grown in it when we visited – they were really good anyhow.

I was fascinated to find you growing in your garden what I thought was giant hogweed *Heracleum mantegazzianum*, a plant we all try desperately to get rid of in England. You corrected me in no uncertain manner telling me it was really the giant cow parsnip and that everybody loves it. My only excuse is that by the time I took a peek at it it was in horrible condition, more or less totally gone over. To you it's a star of the white garden in spring when it blooms. You went into raptures about the great big tropical leaves, these immense toothed things, and were desperately trying to raise enough plants for gifts to keep your admiring neighbours happy. Let me explain my horror. Our giant hogweed has become a pernicious weed in England. It escaped from Kew or Oxford Botanic Garden years ago and is spreading madly along rivers and down roads, probably on car tyres or something. The real problem is that it's got this dangerous toxin that affects the skin (is the world photopathetic?) It bleaches the pigment out of the skin. The danger is if children cut a piece of stem and make a pea-shooter out of it, when they put it to their lips it will damage the pigment of their lips and then they'll get sunburned and get terrible blisters. Now I am home again and have found the time to look up your plant I find that it is by no means poisonous or dangerous. In fact the young stems can be cooked and eaten, although the books tend to warn against eating it in case a wrong identification is made (very sensible). All the same if you can propagate a few maybe you should try boiling it up!

Thinking about weeds, my big fear in tramping about the woods of North America is the dreaded poison ivy. I have seen a sufferer covered in the dreadful boils and sores caused by this plant. It is unknown in Britain, and I hope it is never imported or allowed to escape from some specialist collection to become the scourge of our highways and byways.

When we visited you in the summer, the children went round to those neighbours of yours – sort of down the lane and then turn left – and they had a very nice climbing frame in the garden that came from a Maine company called the Cedar Works. After leaving you we drove up to see them, and they really had a terrific display of first-class climbing frames. We discussed shipping with them, and they came up with a price of just under $2,000 for a really good big unit with about twelve accessories, rings, ropeladders, slippery poles, boat swings, baby swings and more. Back in England we got costings on comparable equipment; the price ran out at about £5,000, four times as much, and the equipment was neither as interesting nor as aesthetically pleasing. What's gone wrong in our poor country?

All this reminds me of the last time we did major work on the children's area. This story will give you some idea of what it's like to run a garden democratically. About six years ago we completely reorganized the play area. It was on a patch of the lawn under a weeping ash and a false acacia where nothing would grow, not even grass; if there were just a few drops of rain, it turned into a mud bath. I decided that it was time we had a more organized play area with a bed of bark mulch for the little devil darlings to fall on. At the same time we were in the process of relaying an adjacent patio. The plan was to lay the patio over the top of what was there, which apart from the main surface of loosely laid crazy paving included two different brick and cement floors (two sheds that were long gone). It took about three man-days a week just to keep the weeds down! We concreted over the whole lot and laid bricks in a series of patterns like a very simple mosaic. The area for the children was dug up and the edges finished off with bricks, it was then filled with grunged up bark to a depth of about eight inches. All this work had been discussed by the democratically elected garden committee, plans had been submitted and budgets drawn up and approved. This was when the trouble started.

A couple who had just moved into the square had been

canvassing for the local Conservative party and thus had made contact with a great many of the residents. They came to the conclusion, for God knows what reason, that rather than trying to improve the garden the garden committee were trying to ruin it. An expression bandied about in reference to the patio was 'helicopter landing pad'. Using their contacts in the square they persuaded seven or eight people to write to the garden committee chairman to protest. She was very upset and felt very insecure about it, leaving me no other option than to ring around some of the residents that use the garden and ask them to write to the chairman expressing their views. In a few days she received more than forty letters, all supporting the new work we were doing. Fine, the committee were happy. Next we had a letter threatening the committee with an injunction for acting illegally! So we had to go to a solicitor, at considerable expense, to get an opinion as to the legal position. He examined the minutes of the committee and found that it had been properly elected, and that all the work had been properly discussed and agreed, all being minuted in an accurate and detailed form. The next move was to report us to our local council for transgressing planning regulations. The planning department telephoned me and asked to come and have a look. The man who came said: 'This is a private garden and as such a structure has to be over five feet tall before planning needs to be applied for.' This however did not seem to satisfy our opponents because a few weeks later I was again contacted by the council rescinding the statement of their officer and saying that the garden was not in fact private but a public garden and that planning consent would therefore be needed. A very contentious statement, as we do not allow public access; legal precedents in the past have referred to these London squares as built strictly as private gardens for the sole use of the residents surrounding them. We were advised, in the event correctly, to ignore the council's contradictory request. Of course one of the side effects was that our local councillors were for a while suspicious of the garden committee, the smear stuck for a bit. Now happily they have had numerous chances of visiting the garden and seeing the work that has been done and the way that it is run. Currently our relationship is very good and the council is very supportive. We have not heard a squeak out of our persecutors for some years now. This will give you a picture of what is involved in running a garden in a city, all the sleep that is lost not over droughts, floods and frosts but over the machinations of the very people whom you are working to help – moan – moan – moan. I hope I am not putting my head back in the lion's mouth by ordering the new Maine play equipment.

Our new book on perennials is just being launched and Martyn and I are being taken for lunch to L'Escargot in Soho, a restaurant that is irresistible not just for the food but for the

wonderful Elena Savloni who is a superb *maître d'*. Never a
face is forgotten – she knows every artist and writer per-
sonally and makes everyone so welcome. Keep up the good
work on your compost.
Love,

Roger

Pleasant Valley, New York

Dear Roger,

Having left off with the outhouse I shall commence at once with the outdoor shower – a triumph of low tech efficiency if ever there was one. (Unlike the Clivus Multrum – Abby Rockefeller's loo, which is unlikely to catch on big not just because it takes quite a while for the fruit fly situation to sort itself out but because it's bloody *huge* and yet designed to go in the house. Well actually the throne itself is regulation but the underlying apparatus . . . after all ours is in the barn.) Anyway, the shower: water supply is a garden hose hooked up to a faucet on the back porch. Lois's son Eli made the heater part out of an old fifty-gallon copper water tank and a pane of glass left over from my little house. (When I put in the back window and skylight I got a deal on some huge (four by five and a half feet) thermopane windows. Several single-thickness pieces came along as part of the package. Very useful.)

Eli built a triangular box, painted the inside black and mounted the black-painted tank at the back. The glass went on as the front panel and the whole thing was mounted on the south-facing edge of the chicken house roof. (No chickens for the last thirty years or so.) It's an ideal spot: the curve of the yard, the big apple tree, and the old outhouse with its vines all screen the west side. On the east there's a dense, ancient lilac. With only a short length of fence the shower area – a simple wooden platform – was made completely private.

It didn't work too well the first year. You could use it only a few hours a day: from 10 to 11.30 a.m. or so and again at about 4.30. The rest of the time you'd have scalded to death. So the next year Eli rigged up a cold tap and now it's perfection, in regular use from mid-June until late September. The bugs are occasionally a problem – have I mentioned the black flies, deer flies and mosquitoes without which no tale of gardening in Maine is even remotely authentic? But other than that all we do is try to remember to use properly biodegradable soap.

As far as I'm concerned the niftiest thing is pure duration. The water's so hot that at midday in midsummer you can take about a forty-five-minute shower just standing there under the warm water looking out over the ravine at the ferns and birches and wild cherries, mosses and spruce trees. The blackberries aren't bothered – if anything, they're encouraged – so in fruiting time you can pick and eat berries while bathing.

Occasionally, you can bat watch, too. Just this last summer I was out there quite late in the season, already early September but still warm. I reached up to adjust the temperature and there was a little face looking down at me from under a loose shingle right below the hot tap. I think the water coming down the pipe must have warmed things up overmuch and forced him to move down, because when I went back later to admire him again he was back well up under the shingle and much harder to see.

Concerning the cow parsnip: I didn't realize I was so defensive but I *am* extremely proud of it. Its tropical gorgeousness won't seem like any big deal to you, but I have a lot of trouble with wide-leaved plants because the garden is so drouthy, so I'm always delighted when I get something to balance all that spiky grey lace. Furthermore I feel very parental because it was a seed-starting success of no mean proportions. I first got interested by reading about it in the J. L. Hudson catalogue, where it was listed as '*Heracleum villosum*, reaching ten feet in height with fragrant, Queen-Anne's-lace-like umbels four feet across'. Clearly worth a try, though they did say the seed had to be stratified. So stratify I did, starting in, I think, January. I planted the seed in moist soil, then froze the pot for six weeks, as per instructions. Then, still following orders, I put said pot where the temperature was approximately 75 degrees. Nothing happened. I tended it all through the early spring, watering sparingly but keeping my eye on it so it never dried out . . . all the boresome usual. When the big spring crunch came in May I began to neglect it and eventually the pot was set aside in the front hall (under the shelf of jam jars) and forgotten.

It was rediscovered the following January, in my approximately once-a-decade thorough house cleaning, and in my more regular house cleaning style set aside to be dealt with later. Then in March when it was time to round up all pots, there it was. So I watered it. Eureka! or not eureka, I guess, but whoopee or something. Sprouts in any event. Which I planted out where they did nothing much but made handsome mounds about three feet around. They wintered over, got bigger, but did not bloom. Finally, in the third summer, giant umbels as promised, albeit only on two of six or seven plants. No fragrance.

Aphids, though. You would not believe how attractive the green seed heads are to aphids. They don't bother the plants or the flowers in bloom, but the seed heads get so covered they're black with the little bastards and unspeakably disgusting if you get close enough to see what's up. This is a great pity as the structure remains dandy even when completely gone by and dried up. It's a mystery, too. Aphids have never been a problem here except on fava beans – even the roses aren't usually bothered. This summer, 1991, it became clear that the cow parsnips die after flowering. Neither of the plants that had bloomed came back. All the others did, but they all *bloomed*, damn 'em, and since I'd lost the little bit of seed that had formed (aphids!) I was afraid I'd lose the lot. But then it turned out that several of the little plants that I thought in spring were self-sown anemones were actually them and *then* I went up to my land on the mountain above the Rockland bog and there was a whole slew of 'em merrily growing in the ditch beside the road. Smaller, less spectacular, but definitely the article. If there's a moral to this tale I'm not sure I want to know it.

The tale of the children's area is – well I was going to say 'simply beyond belief' but of course it's all too believable. It also reminds me to tell you how my little house came to its present location.

Originally an old garage, the building had been moved to the hillside across from Lois's house about forty years ago. There it languished, the scrub growing up around it, until I came along and bought it. Well and good, but I still had to get it to its future home; we had figured out that it ought to be tucked into the slope on the other side of the road about 1200 feet to the northeast. Got estimates from moving companies that pick up houses with cranes and put them on flatbed trucks. Horrendous. Got estimate from a good friend, a lobster fisherman and part time carpenter, who is good at improvised solutions. Much more reasonable. He would jack up the building, which was resting on concrete blocks, set it down on raw spruce skids and then drag it across and down the road. This being winter, it would slide along handily when pulled by his bulldozer, his father's tractor, and the four-wheel drive truck driven by his father's assistant.

I prepared to call around to the planning board, power company and various other interested parties. 'Bad idea,' said my friend. 'Expensive. A hassle. Fuck the permits.' (The correct pronunciation is per-*mits*', accent on the second syllable, and I must tell you this phrase is the Rural New England National Anthem; you shouldn't think our case is unusual.)

The building (eighteen by twenty feet, clapboard, big windows, one and a half stories) was jacked onto the skids without incident. A path was cleared through the nascent forest of poplars and alders. The movers showed up on the appointed day and manoeuvred the building down to the brink of the road. Where it sat, at a 45 degree angle, for approximately an hour while they went off God knows where to have lunch and I sat over at Lois's and had apoplexy. (They had forbidden me to come anywhere near the action.)

After lunch, they sent the luckless assistant to stand on the steep, snow-covered roof with a wooden pole in case he had to push up the power lines so they could squeak under them. You think I am making this up. I am not making this up. I was beside myself but that just made two of me as there was nobody else around. The building grunted onto the some-what icy blacktop, which it pretty much filled both lanes of, and sailed smoothly along without incident for about seventy feet. Then the tractor threw a rod.

It took more than two hours to fix the tractor, during which time I stood at one end of the building and the assistant stood at the other and we waved along the mercifully few passing cars – there was just barely room to squeeze through on one side. All calamity, including the serendipitous advent of any members of the planning board, was miraculously avoided. By the time the house made it across the road it was almost dark, so they didn't bring it to the site until the next day. Then they put it down about 10 degrees off of the angle I had in mind. Wouldn't pick it up and move it, either, although I begged.

Then my friend and I built an addition (ten by twenty-eight feet), at the north end of the building. No permission needed, the house, being on posts, is a movable structure. In fact that was the original idea; neither Lois nor I thought I'd stay when I came. We always figured someday I'd buy my own land and emulate the turtle; the little house is my version of a trailer.

Oh well, Irony Time. The house is staying and I'm going, only not really. I'm seeing this move as First Page of Next

Chapter. Everything is different now that I've fallen for the
entire domestic package: partner, child, dog and cat, a large
rather falling-down house (*two* bathrooms, *no* outhouse) in
the suburbs. I'm still a little stunned to realize I've bought the
whole nine yards. But I'll be in Maine every summer, expect
the garden to gain in structure what it loses in detail as I plant
more shrubbery, rearrange trees, finally plant my lilac hedge.

Of course, how could it be otherwise? Just as I finally learn
how to make the Maine garden less labor intensive, just as the
years of soil-building finally begin to pay off, just as I finally
start to understand the needs of that land and landscape, I get
to start all over in New York. The new property is smaller,
only a bit over an acre all told, but everything that isn't house
is garden, pretty much, and all of the garden is either ancient
and grown over but extremely promising (the grounds of the
house) or totally prospective and a tough row to hoe (the
quarter-acre strip across the road that will be our vegetable
garden but requires considerable work first as it used to be a
railroad bed. You insert your shovel, or try to, and the
ground fights back.)

Bill is an enormous asset. He's a hard worker, loves to
garden, and is remarkably generous about saying 'but this is
really your specialty, dear, just tell me what you want to do
and I'll help you'. The downside of this is that he's not so
much a hard worker as an addicted one. He'll do what I want
if I can figure out what I want, but he won't stand still. He's
not very good at just waiting a minute while I see how it
should go, and if I don't express specific wishes he simply
swashbuckles in there and does what feels right to him,
regardless.

As you know, I'm more the slow type, and I'm especially
eager to go through a full year here just noticing, before I
start what will indeed be a major renovation. The last several
owners of the house have done nothing, but there was a real
gardener here at one time. According to the neighbor's

stories, she was Beatrice (Wells) Allen, the last of the Wells (the road is Wells drive). Her family owned the place from the late 1800s through its whole career as a railroad station (did I mention that it used to be a railroad station?) until about 1980, when the old lady, long since too frail to do any gardening, could no longer keep up the place and had to sell.

Judging from the shrubbery, she was at her most vigorous in the 1940s and 50s, when, as far as I can tell, she bought specimens with mad abandon and then sprinkled them around the yard wherever she saw a space. Jeepers. But I want to try to find her (she's in a nursing home 'somewhere upstate') and find out what I can *before* I start the considerable editing that will be required. Bill understands this, at least in theory, and fortunately he can practise on the vegetable garden when the urge to toil is too strong to resist.

I do already have all sorts of plans, but intend to leave them on paper until I know more. First order of business will be to return to Maine in March and build a (very small) addition on the little house so Bill's daughter Celia will have a room of her own. That loft-like open space was fine when I was by myself. In fact, I loved it, a box of light in a garden.

But now it's time for goodbye to all that – and to you. I'll write more about the new place next time.

Love,

Leslie

3 December 1991

Dear Leslie,

Tomorrow off to New Zealand, for publicity tour for *Perennials*. I have got the most ghastly schedule – pre-breakfast radio then a breakfast including a talk, then on and on and on. But all very exciting. In between I will try to photograph the whole NZ flora for the up and coming books!

Chagrin! England, the country that pioneered health insurance for all and come to that education for all, has finally given up the struggle. Two days ago I was talking to a man who has business in Spain, Germany and England. Under the new European Community laws that come into action in 1992 you cannot have profits in all three countries at once, you have to declare your profit in one or the other. Vipin (that's his name) has discussed it with his accountant and been advised that the best of those three countries to declare profit in – from a tax point of view – is Britain. I am sure that Thatcher would be proud to hear him say it, but I am disgusted, what it means is that we pay less tax and thus have fewer services than anywhere in Europe. All the marvellous work done over the last hundred years, that made us the envy of the world (especially of America) in health care and education – especially for the poor and disadvantaged – has been undermined so that the better off can take home more pay. I am making a considerable saving under our new laws and I hate it. I would be happy to pay more national and local taxes (we used to call them rates), to help the poor sods who ain't got nothin'.

In my latest copy of *The Rose*, the magazine of the rose society, there are two articles about blue roses. Apparently the American company, Jackson and Perkins, are working on altering the genetic structure so that a rose can be grown to any specification including the introduction of animal and even human genes into the strain. This will no doubt mean that we can have a blue rose that smells of lavender that can dance around the garden to the music of an orchestra formed of yet other freaks.

Thirty years ago I saw a film that Jean Paul Sartre had something to do with, about producing hybrid animals – sheep as nimble as goats yet three times as large, pigs crossed with cows to give them an enormous size and other horrors, but after all this time I see no evidence of these monsters in mass production. Let's hope we will be excused having climbing roses with delphinium flowers and delphiniums with rose-scented flowers!

Two key dates in the garden: 1 November the first flower came out on a camellia – *sasanqua* 'Hugh Evans', a small red single, followed very quickly by *sasanqua* 'Narumi Gata', a lovely small cup-shaped white single flower with pink on the outside of the petals. We will now have camellias in flower until the end of next April except if we got a really bad cold spell in which case they will take a couple of weeks off. The second key date is 21 November the first touch of frost on the lawns, just enough to start to kill off the nasturtiums. It's now 1 December and the first lovely scented flowers have appeared on the *Viburnum X bodnantense*.

I will try to write on my antipodean route.

Here is a sketch and plant list for the hellebore bed which is starting to stir – I usually get a few flowers by Christmas.

Lots of love to you both,

Roger

BED 14
The Winter Bed

SCALE 1mm = 10cm (1/100)

BED 14: THE WINTER BED

SHRUBS

A = *Acacia baileyana*
B = *Betula jaquemontii*, the Himalayan birch
C = *Camellia* 'Contessa Lavinia Maggi'
D = *Camellia* 'Cornish Spring'
E = *Camellia* 'Grace Bunton'
F = *Hamamelis × intermedia* 'Arnold Promise'
G = *Hamemalis × intermedia* 'Jelena'
H = *Prunus glandulosa sinensis*

I = *Prunus mume Benichidori*
J = *Syringa vulgaris*
K = *Viburnum opulus Sterile*
L = *Viburnum plicatum Mariesii*

PERENNIALS

M = *Artemisia absinthinum* 'Lambrook Silver'
N = *Calamintha grandiflora*
O = *Digitalis lutea*
P = *Helleborus corsicus*
Q = *Helleborus foetidus*
R = *Helleborus foetidus* 'Western Fisk'
S = *Helleborus niger*
T = *Helleborus orientalis*, many forms
U = *Iris florentina*
V = *Iris germanica*
W = *Symphytum* 'Hidcote Pink', comfrey
X = *Symphytum* × *uplandicum*, *Variegatum*, the variegated comfrey
Y = *Viola odorata*

There are also annual Opium Poppies, Wild Larkspur, Godetia and clumps of Carex pendula, *that self-seed and come up in any open patches.*

Pleasant Valley, N.Y.

December 16, 1991

What can I say, Roger? Oh, to be in England, where the flowers bloom all year! Nasturtium-killing frost came to New York in late September, it feels like eons ago. So far we've had precious little snow but the growing season is definitely over for at least a couple of months. *Our* key dates have been October 26, when Bill went out to the swamp behind the garden and shot (with bow and arrow) a large deer that will provide our winter meat; November 25, when I finally got the last of 22 big clumps of peonies out from under the overgrown lilacs and into safekeeping behind the vegetables; and December 4, when we discovered froggie hiding in the Christmas cactus.

I'm not much of a houseplant fan so all we have are a few odds and ends: A 'Red Planet' fibrous begonia that has refused to die for so long it's become part of the family, a bucket of pink cannas that were still going strong when I packed up the Maine garden for the winter, a potful of *Asarina scandens* that moved indoors without complaint when winter arrived, and (point of story) the good sized *Schlumbergera* × *buckleyi* that old Mrs Katsaros, Peter's mom, gave Bill as a house-warming gift.

Pace houseplants, one good thing to be said for epicacti is they don't need much attention, and not much attention is just what we've bestowed on Mrs K's present. But then that day I was peering at it – rather balefully, only one or two buds and here comes Christmas so maybe in spite of the floppy joints it's actually *Rhipsalis gaertneri* and won't do anything till Easter – when I saw a tiny frog crouched down near the base of the plant. It blinked, bubbled out its throat, and turned its head ever so slightly. I stared. Called the

197

family. We stared. It bubbled its throat. End of interaction. Succeeding days have been just the same. He's cute, but he ain't lively.

Evidently, he's been with us since September, minding his (or her, it's impossible to tell) own business and we've never heard a peep out of him. So although he's probably an *Hyla versicolor*, the Common Grey Tree Frog, he *might* be *H. chrysoscelis*, Cope's Grey Treefrog. According to the Audubon Field Guide, the two species can only be told apart by their songs and their chromosome counts. Whatever he is, he's about the size of a quarter (4.5 cm) and either a sort of mottled pewter or a bright, rather bluish green depending on what he's been sitting on.

The book says 'they live high in trees and descend only at night, usually just to chorus and to breed'. Poor froggie, precious little of either *he's* enjoying. Bill had frogs in his greenhouse over on Verbank Road, and he says the beastlet will do fine until spring (when we'll let him go) with no help from us, but I think we'd better feed him. I gave him a couple of moth larvae – from a box of crackers that had become infested in the back reaches of the pantry closet – and they were very warmly engulfed.

Spring seems far away. There's not much we can do right now but prune a bit and plan a lot. For starters we have fenced the vegetable gardens, a pair of fifty-foot squares in the center of the lot across the roadway. Right now it's just wire mesh to keep out rabbits, dogs, and the less enterprising deer, but there's white picket to come. Everything in the neighborhood – or, more accurately, everything attractive – is mid-late Queen Anne or Mansard, white with black or green shutters and trim, so there isn't a lot of leeway in the design department. A real change from Maine: if it ain't regular, it ain't right. Even Bill, whose tastes incline to the picturesque, agrees.

He's at work building a new arbor to replace the falling

down one. The new version will be slightly larger, even closer to the Eastern edge of the property, and quite a bit taller, all with an eye toward privacy enhancement. Our neighbor's drive is right on *her* side of the line, and there's no cover other than the lilacs. In time, there will be tall evergreens (uninspired but necessary; that way also lies a loud highway).

Meanwhile, grapes should help do the job; this seems to be an ideal climate for them in spite of the summer heat (and the Japanese beetles). Last year the present incumbents made a huge thicket even though there are only two vines: a Concord and a seedless white that's probably Interlaken. Unpruned since Eden, they both have long, gnarley trunks and multiple arms. And both, contrary to all received wisdom, last year bore enormous crops that were mostly enjoyed by the birds. My guess is that they were planted in the fifties.

No knowing when the bittersweet came, but the evil stuff sure is well established, hideously robust, *everywhere*. It's woven in all of the flower beds, sprouting forth among the raspberries, waving in tall plumes high above the 50 foot juniper next to the carriage house. Bill gets periodic fits of bittersweet removal mania, but I just try to yank up a bit whenever I'm near one, on the 'no flies in China' theory. 'No' is not to be, of course, bittersweet is the kudzu of the North. Or the sort-of-North. By the time you get to New England, it's not nearly as much of a problem.

Same, alas, with the poison ivy, a scourge scarcely known in Maine that's more or less endemic here. I'm still not used to it. At Thanksgiving I almost picked several branches of the lovely ivory berries to decorate the house, was saved only by vine-recognition at the very last minute. Mercifully, there are zillions of hairy little rootlets that grow all over the trunks of older specimens, and this unmistakable feature provides a most welcome warning.

The sneezeweed, completely unknown in Maine, is quite

Berries green in summer white in winter

POISON IVY

The leaves up trees are less cut

The leaves near the ground are more deeply cut

pretty and easy to pluck up, unlike the ladies' bedstraw, which is quite pretty and not so easy to pluck up. The roots are right at the surface, but matty, and you never get them all. There's onion grass, too. Lots of onion grass. I see in *Wild Food* that all the wild alliums are edible. Where have I gotten this dim memory that there is a poisonous one, or a poisonous look/smell-alike? Our lawns and gardens are full of the stuff. Again, nothing like it in Maine.

I never dreamed the look, feel, smell, light of the place would be so foreign when so much is familiar. The difference

between an evergreen-dominated treescape (Maine's sob-
riquet is 'The Pine Tree State') and this domain of oak and
maple, locust and sycamore is enough to make being in New
York like being in a far-off country, even though I haven't so
much as left my home climate zone. New Zealand seems
almost unimaginable, and Christmas in New Zealand an
adventure indeed.

We had the tree-trimming party just last night, having
gotten the guest of honor at the last minute, the day before
yesterday. Bill and Celia went out in a rainstorm to their
friend John Forman's place, where there's a forest of overgrown Christmas trees that were somehow or other left
unharvested until long past saleability. B. climbed a very
large fir, cut off the top twenty feet or so, and brought the
top twelve of that home. We further reduced it to seven and a
half feet and in it came, without breaking anything *mirabile
dictu*.

Celia had two of her friends over and we had a quartet of
Bill's dear old pals: Gil and Margaret Nyhoff and Sue Hart
and her partner, Jim Flynn. Like N.Y. itself, all was the same
yet different. I made the gingerbread disks with blackstrap
molasses this year – an accident that yielded gorgeous color
(very dark and glistening) but did little for taste (bitter and
dull). So the ornaments were strictly for show.

But having them icing painted by the children was a
definite plus, as were the kids themselves – talk about a great
time with the mistletoe! Jim, who is an architect, has the same
precision of technique as my friend Chris. And a new ritual is
in the making now that Celia is part of my life.

Last year when I was first getting to know her I gave her a
Christmas ornament – just because it was pretty. This year, I
got her some tiny brass French horns, a salute to her growing
skill on that difficult instrument. Next year who knows, but
there will be something. She's nine now, so by the time she's
ready to set up housekeeping she'll have a nice little collection

to hang on her own tree, pretty mementoes of Christmases past to help make a new place home.

I've certainly brought enough baggage here with that same end in mind; my grandmother's rocker for the living room, sage from Maine for hedging what we've taken to calling the garden of unknown roses. It seems to be working. The black hollyhocks look as good against the walls of this big white house as they did against the weathered grey ones of the little cottage. Turnabout being fair play, I plan to bring several clumps of New York's overabundant *tradescantia* to Maine, expect them to look right at home in the blue border.

Now I feel as well as understand the impulse to lilacs that moved the pioneers, now know that it was more than simply wanting to have lilacs when they got there. You take fuller possession of new ground when you grow old plants in it, prove to your heart that you too can thrive on unfamiliar soil.

I reread your letter and think of those less fortunate – almost everybody – and What Is To Be Done! And then I too think gardening is more fun and then I feel guilty and *then* I think: Well, wait a minute. The big problems: poverty, wars, the whole caboodle, all boil down in the end to one basic question: who gets to eat good food, breathe clean air and smell a few flowers in peace? And the answer is going to be 'nobody', if we don't get our ecological act together.

So we might as well start in the garden, where the few home truths that have widest application are (are they ever!) ever-present: only the energy of the sun is limitless; balance is essential; human intervention is both inevitable and okay. The human hand, eye, mind and heart are also part of the garden, as natural as spruce trees, as lions and tigers, as swamp mud and weeds.

If I understand your travel plans correctly, Christmas will be history by the time you read this. But we'll have been thinking of you on the day, and again at midnight on the 31st when we plan to follow what I believe is an old Viennese custom. As the clock strikes 12, we will all hold hands and jump off the couch as far as we can – away from the troubles of the past and into the New Year.

Until then,

Best Love
Leslie

ECCLESTON SQUARE,
LONDON

15 January 1992

Dear Leslie,

The trip to the Antipodes was mind boggling: thousands of plants so different from our northern things, it's like being lost in a vast ocean of plants without a chart.

I started out in Auckland by visiting a man with a native plant nursery, called Graeme Platt. After about half an hour poking about in the nursery he proposed taking me out into the last area of native rainforest left in the Auckland district. I was dressed for mid-summer, just shorts and T-shirt, everyone having told me how dreadfully hot it would be. Wrong, I was absolutely frozen. As soon as we got to the rainforest it started chucking it down and in two minutes I was a crawling sponge.

One of the things I had planned to shoot in New Zealand was a group of wild tree ferns for the forthcoming *Annuals* book. Back in England I had done quite a bit of research to make sure that I would be able to find a good site. Wrong again. They were everywhere, virtually pushing up between the paving stones, covering old railway embankments and battling their way back towards the greens of a recently opened golf course. Apart from the rain and the cold it was very dull and dark which made photography incredibly difficult; I had to hand-hold at one eighth of a second at f3.5 (the only way to do that is to lean the camera against a tree or a log).

Apart from the stunning ferns, tree and giant ground (or should they be called shrub) ferns, the most remarkable thing was the giant kauri trees. The trunks are totally round and perfectly straight for about the first fifty feet without a single branch, then they continue up to a good two hundred and fifty feet and, like everything else down there, they are evergreen. They must be like a dream come true to a logger because the diameter of the trunk is something like sixteen feet, all of it excellent wood, for although they live to as much as 3000 years, they get very little heart rot. Graeme has been studying the way they grow all his life and has, in the last ten years or so, been able to start a breeding programme.

Firstly, he selects the best specimens in the forest, then he collects the seeds suspended from a helicopter! Getting seedlings started is not a problem but getting them to grow well has been the sticking point. Graeme's solution is not to dig holes and plant them in the soil but to put them down on top of the soil and spread out the roots and then cover them with rotted forest leaf mould. Of course you have to keep them very wet. It works like a dream; his three-year-old plants were putting on about three feet of growth a year. As far as I could see this growth was due to the mycorhizal symbiosis of the fungi that were rotting down the leaf litter. Even if mycorhizal fungi were not the mystery ingredient it must have been leaf-rotting fungi breaking down the leaf litter that supplied them with their nutrients.

After drying out there was a little reception in the hotel in Auckland, the address of which mystified me – 'Private Bag'. Is it a reference to their clients? We drank delicious local Chardonnay, but, and this is what I was knocked out by, we ate Kumara chips; to us in England they would be 'crisps'. Anyway, they were made from sweet potatoes, the big round yellowish type with yellow flesh. In New Zealand they call them golden Kumara. It was my gastronomic treat of the whole trip.

Many radio shows later (New Zealanders are very passionate about radio) I went to see Sam McGredy, the great rose breeder, the fourth Sam McGredy in line from the Irish rose breeders of Portadown. Twenty years ago Sam moved to New Zealand and has found the climate perfect for roses. 'I feel sorry for my old friends back in Europe spending money on greenhouses and then having to pay to heat them as well,' he said. Sam was terrific company, a great bear of a man with bristling grey hair and the strength and energy to carry the world's rose production on his back. He had kept back, to show me, the flowers on his latest crop of seedlings, fifty thousand bred from seven thousand crosses, this meant I could see them in all their glory. After I left all the flowers were to be cut and chucked out and about sixty per cent of the plants would be discarded also. Eventually he hopes that about four from this massive programme would come into cultivation. His passion of the moment? Sam believes that the Hybrid Tea is the way to go. He feels breeders have neglected them in recent years – thus few excellent Hybrid Tea roses have been bred and the public have started buying Floribundas and Old Roses. Sam is trying to develop some new striped Hybrid Tea varieties for the future.

Down to the South Island, more radio, etc. but on my last day I got the chance to go up in the high alpine mountain area with a local expert plantsman, Derek Rooney. We went up from sea level to about eight thousand feet, the snow line. The mountains are incredibly young in geological terms. Mount Cook is getting taller at the rate of about a quarter of an inch a year. Being so young, the higher areas have no soil at all: the slopes consist almost entirely of scree. We left Derek's Land-Rover and climbed up steep cliffs for an hour or two, finding the most extraordinary plants, me photographing desperately as we went until I sat down to look at a flower and the camera tipped out of my bag and started on a thousand-foot journey to the bottom of the scree and total destruction.

A New Zealand fact. There are only two native mammals, both bats!

Now Australia. Cars and trucks have bars on the front

here, called roo bars. At night kangaroos leap into the road
and then stand still in the lights. I am sure the bars are the
same as Americans sometimes have to protect themselves
against leaping deer. The only wild kangaroo I saw was a
dead one on the roadside when I drove from Sydney to
Canberra to see the Australian National Botanic Gardens.
The long drive was well worth it, about two hundred acres of
native plants set in a completely natural eucalyptus forest
setting. I wandered around totally out of my depth amongst
plants and forms absolutely new to me. I was conscious
enough to shoot about twenty rolls of film though.

Christmas Day this year we spent on the beach of Morn-
ington Peninsula, just south of Melbourne; it was a blissful 80
degrees, we had a small barbecued turkey (cold) which we
tore to bits with our fingers. Phoebe went fishing – her
new-found passion. That day she caught nothing but two
days later we got up at dawn and had another try and she
caught a Japanese blow fish. I didn't know what it was and
we would have eaten it and probably died the instant death
that the Japanese go in for every year, if we had not boasted
of our catch to a local in the hotel who was able to put a name
to it and warn us off it. On Boxing Day I went to see the
cricket – the first day of a five-day Test match, Australia v.
India, at the MCG (Melbourne Cricket Ground). Australia
has a terrific tall lanky bowler called Reed who tore through
the Indian batsmen. No doubt I have lost you. The last time I
took an American to see cricket he could not believe how one
game could last five days.

After Melbourne we flew to Perth. I was very excited to
get amongst the wild flowers but January is really too late in
the season, early September would be better. Never mind. I
found more than I could take in. I drove north about a
hundred miles up into the bush. It is astounding; miles and
miles of shrubby woods consisting mainly of banksias with
the occasional bright yellow grevillea poking out above

them. I managed to get the car stuck up a dirt road and was just contemplating survival without water in near desert conditions – could I eat the giant fat lizards that were all over the place when a truck pulled up, the driver jumped out with a heavy-duty chain and pulled me out. 'G'day,' he said. 'You could have been here for days. I am the only fella ever uses this track.'

Back in England everything seems very small and old-fashioned. As a nation we have totally failed to invest in our future. I feel that it is most depressing: unless something radical happens we will become a very minor museum with our only asset our tourism. Oh well, maybe that will be better than the brash world motivated only by more money that I have seen so much of on this trip. Singapore for instance looked as if it handled as much shipping, or more, than all the ports in Britain put together.

Fujita, the people who got me to plan that garden square, are holding fire on the laying out of the Loudon garden. I suppose even the Japanese fear recession. What a shame. It was a real chance to do something with historical significance.

The first camellias are bursting into bloom – it's going to be a bumper crop. There are about twice as many buds as ever before!

Love,

Roger

P.S. Yes, I would love some morning glory seeds. I am desperate for good ones this year. Do you still have them?

THREAT TO LONDON SQUARES

London Square Gardens are increasingly coming under threat from developers who are pressurizing the city planners to grant planning permission to build car parks under them.

The sole purpose of the Society is to protect London Squares from any such development.

Whilst we all appreciate the enormous transport problems in London the idea of destroying the very character of our city by turning square gardens into semi-industrial sites must be totally repugnant to those of us who live in the capital. The property companies, under the guise of providing a solution to London's parking problem, are in a position to exert enormous pressure on planners at both borough and government level. They also have the financial means to put enormous resources behind any such proposals; profits from building one car park could amount to between five and thirty million pounds.

The Society objects to the building of such car parks in the centre of London. They would inevitably lead to even worse traffic congestion, increase air and noise pollution, create an environment conducive to crime and irretrievably damage the square gardens which make such an important contribution to the environmental balance of our city.

Attempts to resolve this situation politically; the amendment to the London Squares Preservation Act (1931) proposed by Dudley Fishburn M.P. (Kensington), and the amendment to the London Local Authorities Act (No. 2), seem destined to failure. Both Local Authorities and Central Government are wary of totally legislating against underground developments which would preclude any future works they might deem to be of pre-emptive importance.

Therefore the defence of London Squares against developers searching only for profit without any thought of the environment, will have to be conducted by those who love and cherish the unique heritage of gardens and squares that characterize our city. No Garden Square can easily fight this battle alone. As you may have seen in our letter published in *The Times* 29 November 1989, we have therefore formed:

THE SOCIETY FOR THE PROTECTION OF LONDON SQUARES

The plan is for the society to gather together knowledge, expertise and experts so that there will be a repository of information and addresses of concerned bodies and individuals.

Roger Phillips
Hon. Chairman